_ S 4 R

S W
R

800-737-8866

LIVE
CAMP
WORK

How to Make Money While Living in an RV & Travel Full-Time.

_ A L I D

Sharee Collier

L A D L _

S O A R ___

o

BA __ _ R

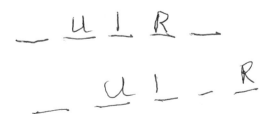

_ u l R _

_ u l _ R

This book is dedicated to my loving family. Without you there would be no family adventure or wild travel tales of a life spent living on the road free to roam. Thank you for always supporting my crazy ideas! Especially the one when I said, 'Let's live in an RV!' Without you this book would not be possible!

I love you to the moon and back-

Acknowledgements

I can't thank my family enough for their support along this RV adventure and for their flexibility, love and encouragement. This book would not have been possible, if it weren't for their understanding of the extensive hours of pouring my heart and soul into projects such as this.

I need to give a special thanks to everyone in my life who has supported my wild ideas especially the dedicated group of fellow Workampers who helped me bring the final product to market. I asked for your comments, thoughts and suggestions and you graciously supplied me with genuine insights that helped me mold the final book. This kind of support is only available from inside the RV community!

Thank you all so much!

Bonus Offer

Thanks so much for purchasing my book, *Live. Camp. Work!*

I appreciate your support and welcome you to research this RV lifestyle further and explore how Workamping can help get you on the road faster!

As an added bonus I would like to give you my **7 Day Workamping Mini Course** for FREE!

This course is just 7 quick modules to get you started on the fast track plus a list of 100 employers who hire RVers.

Head over to www.LiveCampWork.com to grab yours now and get started today!

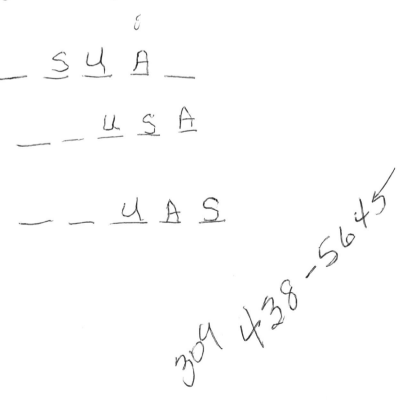

_ E _ _ E _ L

E _ _ _ E L
G

American

Flight #1987

#1540

Table of Contents

Prologue

Hey! I'm Sharee Collier. My husband Antwon and I have been traveling for the past 5 years with our 4 great kids trying to see and do as much as possible on a super road trip we started back in 2013!

Non-traditional life for us started a few years before that, back in 2010 to be exact. Back then we did what everybody else did. Our kids were in a traditional school. We worked 9-5 jobs. We lived in a house, had 2 cars, a dog... the boring list goes on and on. But we woke up one day with the idea to stop. Stop trying to fit in. Stop trying to get 1st place in the rat race. Stop living inside the box. We woke up and wanted nothing more than to just get out and explore.

We made a short list of 3 possible adventures

1. Live at the beach.
2. Live in an RV.
3. Live on a sailboat.

We started with #1 of course! We loved it. The kids loved it. We could walk through the sand dunes to the water in 2 minutes and be back home for lunch or dinner just as quick. Then one day, the kids were literally swimming with sharks. Then another day Antwon almost got washed into the water with the car with the first day of hurricane season. Then one day, shortly after, we decided we were really landlubbers and that water was not comforting!

We looked for an RV and bought one. We did a quick rehab, since ours was actually older than either of us and then moved in! Simple right?

Well, sort of! I mean it wasn't as difficult as many people make it out to be, and to be honest we wouldn't have made it work without the concept of Workamping… that's where you work while you RV, you know so you can keep a steady flow of income as you explore this country (basically- what this whole book is about)! Workamping is a simple idea that so many people have a hard time grasping! It leaves so much for the individual to decide upon and design for themselves, that many people get overwhelmed with the possibilities and the freedom to use it as you wish. After spending 5 years Workamping in various forms as well as the past 2 years behind the scenes as the Director of Operations of the mother company, Workamper News- I think it's time I give a more detailed explanation of the lifestyle for those who are just tuning in!

In *Live.Camp.Work!* I'd like to help clarify common misconceptions that plague the minds of many people considering whether or not Workamping can help them hit the road sooner than retirement, post-retirement, or when retirement isn't even in sight! I'd like to provide some necessary information about the Workamping community and the variety of employment opportunities that are available.

If you'll keep an open mind and a positive outlook, I'll walk you through the basics, dive into the types of jobs available with specific employers, and even provide a list of 1000 employers who hire Workampers in the US to get you started on your adventure faster than you dreamed.

Let's not waste any time…

Let's just get started!

Part 1: Workamping Basics

If you haven't heard by now, Workamping is the adventurous life of work and RV travel! It has grown in popularity over the past decade and stories of its alternative lifestyle have made news headlines from the Seattle Times to the Huffington Post and even a segment on NBC's Today Show!

Media and news reports say people are turning to alternative ways of living and RVing is at the top of the list. More and more people are RVing in the US than ever before and while most people hear the word Workamp and immediately think of retirees, it's not always the case. People who Workamp come from a variety of backgrounds, ethnicities and age demographics and have all taken kindly to the RVing lifestyle for the vast benefits it affords them.

Creators of the popular term, Workamper News, define Workampers as "adventuresome individuals, couples, and families who have chosen a wonderful lifestyle that combines ANY kind of part-time or full-time work with RV camping."

With such a broad definition there is bound to be some confusion and general questions that everyone will want to know the answers to. In this section of the book, I'll walk you through Workamping Basics discussing what exactly all this means for RV travelers.

1: What is Workamping

Every time I mention the word Workamping to a group of people, there is always someone in the group who looks confused by what I'm talking about. There is also always someone ready to help explain the details and how it's really just for retirees, which is just not accurate.

To make it simple, I usually interrupt and start from the top. While I would love to save myself the trouble of explaining that Workamping is not just for retirees, I figure the more folks I talk to, the faster word will spread. So, I might as well start from the top!

An Evolution in Process

Back in 1987, Workamper News was founded by a husband and wife duo who discovered a small group of retired professionals taking short-term positions as they traveled across the country and felt moved to provide a resource to help bring the jobs to the people who wanted them. They coined the word, added a trademark and as a result, the lifestyle of working as you travel would continue to develop and attract the attention of seniors across the map.

For many years the world of Workamping would continue to grow and develop as more and more people took their retirement on the road and worked as camp hosts at various state, national and private campgrounds across the US. So, yes, it all started with retirees and camp hosting positions, but as we all know… times change and so has Workamping.

Naturally, Workamping has evolved to fit the needs and wants of the RV community over the past 30 years. What was once mostly retirees taking their funds on the road for adventures at the best national parks throughout the land, has now turned into one of the fastest growing alternative lifestyles the US has ever seen. Workamping now includes a growing population of younger campers from ages 18 – 55. Many, who have no desire of the traditional life of 9-5 jobs, spending countless hours commuting to work, yard work on the weekends or quietly reading about amazing places in great books by the fireplace. These folks want to see and do as they please, blow into a new destination and conquer all it has to offer, then blow out again just like a cool summer breeze. These are the folks who are shaking up the traditional and bringing Workamping into the future.

With all of this in mind, you might still be wondering, "What is Workamping?" and for you my inquisitive friend, I'd like to offer a simple answer… anything you want!

RV + Work = Travel

Workamping can literally be anything you want it to be. For my family, we started with a dream of exploring the United States. Goals of taking our kids on an endless adventure where small and big discoveries would roll seamlessly into everyday life and family memories would easily be attained through cherished moments together as perpetual travelers.

We fell into Workamping after a few internet searches of 'working + RVing' and came across a program called Camperforce by retail giant Amazon.com.

Working for Camperforce is probably the farthest you can get from the traditional expectation of Workamping, which for us seemed perfect for young folks just starting out, but like many others we would soon figure out that this gig is hard work and takes more than just the ability to stand for extended periods of time, to make it through and still keep your smile! (We'll talk more about this later.)

So back to my original point, if you live in an RV, regardless of if you are full-time, part-time or seasonal and you work, then you are Workamping.

Examples of Workamping

- Volunteering as a Docent or Camp Host
- Selling Campground Maps & Advertising
- Mystery Shopping at Local Businesses
- Operating a Small Business
- Selling Crafts at Fairs & Festivals
- Working as an RV Inspector
- Being a Wagon Master for RV Caravans
- Providing Security at an Oil Field Gate
- Inspecting Gas Lines in Neighborhoods

Since Workamping can be so inclusive, it's best to be broken down into smaller categories that make it easier to follow. I like to think of it in terms of Seasonal Jobs (the largest and most advertised), Location Independent Jobs, Small Businesses & Traditional Jobs.

Seasonal Jobs

The majority of Workamping job opportunities fit into the category of seasonal jobs. They benefit both the employer and the Workamper from this perspective.

> *Employers* are looking for the perfect hires! They need a specific number of reliable employees to come help them out in their busy seasons and then leave when the season is over.

> *Workampers*, on the other hand, want to stay in the best locations during the high seasons and leave when the weather turns to the undesirable type and make some cash to cover expenses.

The intersection where the needs and wants of both parties meet is the picture-perfect place where happy Workampers & employers thrive inside the Workamping community!

Why Choose a Seasonal Job?

Choosing to work in locations during what is considered the Workamping season, or any season for that matter, is a decision to stay put for a specific amount of time. For some, the thought of traveling to a job with the requirement of living in the location for 3-6 months is madness. For others, who see the benefits of traveling slow and working along the way, it brings a variety of adventures season after season.

Since seasonal jobs are the most widely advertised positions, they are also the easiest type of Workamping job to find and acquire. Job sites across the web are filled with advertisements asking Workampers to fill a variety of positions ranging from Site Hosts to Ranch Hands and from Front Desk & Reservations to Grounds Maintenance & Housekeeping.

What Kinds of Jobs are Available?

In a seasonal position, you will have the ability to stay in awesome locations and destinations some people can only dream about spending more than a few days! These locations can include State & National Parks, like Yellowstone or Glacier. It could also mean working more physical positions like Amazon Camperforce and the Sugar Beet Harvest to meet savings goals to travel for the remaining six months out of the year without much need for other gigs.

Positions range from one end of the spectrum to the other and include everything from those mentioned above to food service, housekeeping, working at shooting ranges, activity planning, membership sales, events, festivals and much more.

36 Seasonal Workamping Jobs

1. Gate Guarding
2. On-Site Security Personnel

3. Tour Guide

4. Ski Resort Staff

5. Rafting Tour Guide

6. Volunteer in State Parks

7. National Park General Staff

8. Historical Docent

9. Off- Season Property Caregiver

10. Christmas Tree Lot Managers

11. Pumpkin Lot Managers

12. Firework Sales

13. Dog Show Judge

14. Amusement Park Staff

15. Casino Staff

16. Bus/Shuttle Driver

17. Sporting Event Staff

18. Playing Santa Claus

19. RV Caravan Wagon Master

20. RV Deliveries

21. Visitor Center Worker

22. Maintenance

23. Mystery Shopper

24. Circus Workers

25. RV Inspectors

26. NASCAR Circuit Workers

27. Horse Wrangler

28. Backcountry Patrol

29. Park or Gate Attendant

30. Census Taker

31. Tax Preparer

32. Warehouse Worker

33. Festival Booth Setup

34. Craftsperson

35. Harvest Employee

36. Park Ranger

Many Workamping jobs do not require extensive skills or certifications. Most of the positions advertised can be done by just about anyone with a can-do attitude, a willingness to help in more than one area, and a flexible schedule. To be successful and find jobs easily, you will need a new outlook on what jobs you find attractive. In exchange for a life of travel that allows you to go now rather than later, you will need to figure out what you are willing to do and not do.

Location Independent

A new catchy type of job category we've seen spike in recent years, thanks to the digital era and the love of mobile technology, are location independent jobs.

What is Location Independence?

It means that you can work from anywhere! Location independence is the ability of not having to stay in one location for any specific amount of time or for any reason.

As you can imagine, this is a very attractive category of jobs! Many people who dream of a life full of travel, actually have their sights set on location independence, where they wander freely from place to place, working whenever and wherever they see fit. I'll admit, the life of a location independent nomad with no ties to geography or agreements to work in one location for set amounts of time, with ample time to explore the surround areas at a whim, is pretty awesome, but does seem less attainable for the majority of people.

While location independent jobs are all the rave on social media right now, they can be more difficult to secure if you do not have a background in technology, sales, or even customer service. These positions can vary from a range of tech support careers to customer service representatives and even direct sales positions. They may not be for everyone, but they offer benefits that are very attractive to RVers wishing for a freer style of travel.

Small Businesses

One of the best ways to hit the road with little to no strings attached is to own and operate your very own small business from the comfort of your RV. Small Business owners across the country are finding that RV life affords them the comforts of home, a stable office environment and the freedom to roll wherever the road leads! Running a small business is hard work but can be a very rewarding career strategy for those who have the entrepreneurial spirit and the drive to make it all happen.

Since running a small business from your RV can include just about any business, or hobby for that matter, as long as you are able to generate a steady income stream, the options are limitless.

Some folks start with a hobby they love and turn it into a revenue stream after investing some time and energy to build a client/customer list that can sustain them as they travel. Others find it easier to start a small business and build it around the direct sales or affiliate marketing concepts.

However you find is the best way to build a business you can run from the road, I would recommend you do so. I love the idea of having multiple income streams and while your business may not be able to fully fund your travel and cover all your expenses from the start, it can add extra cash to the pot. As it grows, the revenue and freedom to set and exceed your own goals, make the big decisions, and the ability to do what you love are unmatched by any career.

Traditional Jobs

When I speak of traditional jobs, I'm referring to jobs for companies that do not offer a campsite or make any reference in their hiring or recruiting strategies to hiring RV workers in particular. These companies generally are just looking to hire from the local employment pool and have no interest in how or where you might reside. They either stumble across the Workamper niche and decide hiring a mobile workforce is a great new idea or you find them. In either case, the reasons for and benefits of working such a job can only be measured on a case-by-case basis.

Traditional jobs can include retail positions, tech companies, customer service, call centers, maintenance jobs and anything else you can dream of. The only way they fit into the conversation of Workamping is that you are living in an RV while you work.

With a general understanding of what Workamping is and what types of Workamping jobs are available, let's go on to Chapter 2 where we will make sure to dig into the top four questions pertaining to living in an RV and working while you travel!

2: *Workamping Questions*

There are many questions pertaining to the lifestyle of Workamping, but in this chapter I'm going to tackle the top four. By diving into why people Workamp, where you can go, what you can do, and how much you can make, my goal is to provide you with vital information from the very beginning. After all, it's usually helpful to know the backstory before you dive head first into something!

Why Do People Workamp?

The number one reason people decide to go Workamping is freedom. Freedom of location that is! Freedom of location is basically the ability to not be fully confined by a specific geographic area for one reason or another. It allows ordinary people, like you and me, to explore and create adventures they would not typically be able to have if they worked a regular job and stayed in one place all year long. Similar to location independence, but different in that freedom of location allows for more seasonal moves, with some independence, but not total.

Workamping gives people from all walks of life, all backgrounds and all socioeconomic backgrounds and ethnicities the ability to travel. With the nomadic roots of the Workamping lifestyle, you are instantly able to go wherever you want, do whatever you want and stay as long as you want as long as you can find an employment opportunity that fits. Doesn't that sound awesome?

Ditching the Norm

When my family first set out to RV in 2013, this was advantage number one on our list! We wanted to explore! We wanted to see the other 49 states and we wanted to be able to do it with four kids in tow while making money along the way. Workamping allowed us to check all those boxes and thus we pegged it as our ticket to travel!

For five years, it has led us down some pretty amazing roads and to and from some awesome adventures. Without the ability to work in various locations, which ultimately led to a location independent position with Workamper News, we would still be living the *standard American life,* without knowing if that's truly what we wanted. Workamping gave us the option to choose for ourselves and decide as we saw fit. It can do the same for you.

Many people I've met along our journey have had similar tales- they wanted to do something adventurous for a while, usually saying they would RV for 1 year as a break. They wanted to exit the rat race and live a little. They decided to put those lifelong careers on hold for a year and explore. Some knew from the start they never wanted to return to their sticks and bricks (traditional housing) but they were apprehensive about how it would all work out in the end.

The Workamping lifestyle gave them a chance to ditch it all, start something fresh and full of adventures, and the ability to do it now rather than later. They liked the Workamping lifestyle because it allowed them to start sooner than the typical retirement age and they could do it for as long or as short of a time span as they wished.

The Perks

We've met people who have worked along the way for 20+ years and have no desire to stop any time soon. They have incredible adventures, and many will tell you amazing stories about being able to live in places like Yellowstone National Park for 6 months out of the year! That's insane… Do you know how much it would cost to rent a campsite in Yellowstone for 6 months? We're talking thousands of dollars! But these people didn't have to pay that type of money for their sites. They were Workamping for the National Park Service and their campsites were heavily discounted at about $30 a week plus they were being paid for all hours worked! You can't beat it!

Can you imagine being a snowbird at the age of 24? 37? 48? Even 55 was a bit of a stretch before the world of Workamping was so widely accepted in the past several years! But now the door is open for everyone. That means, for me at least, I can enjoy my ideal temperature range all year long! Cool summers, warm winters and tons of tourist attractions to keep us all busy are just a few of the reasons why people choose to Workamp. You decide for yourself.

Where Can I Go?

This is an easy one... you can go anywhere in the U.S. as a Workamper! You can also go to Canada and Mexico if you are so inclined, but you won't be working in those locations. Maybe start in the east and drive out to the wild wild west. How about starting in the north and then driving all the way down I-95 to Key West for the winter? There's no right or wrong way to travel and you can define your route as you see fit! The question is where do you want to go! Or maybe where have you never been?

An Easy Option

Perhaps the easiest way to figure out where you want to go is by starting with your favorite part of the country. Think about places you've taken trips to and really wanted to stay for more time. Think about those hot tourist destinations you've read about in travel magazines at the grocery store and always dreamed of going. Think about family and friends you wished you could visit and spend more time with on birthdays, holidays and seasons in general! These are the places you should be going as a Workamper! Figure this out and you've just started the first step in planning your adventure! You'll also be one step closer to getting on the road and making money while you travel.

Workamping can provide you with a reliable income and decreased expenses for you to be able to make these special trips to places you've always dreamed of going. And this is exactly how Workampers should plan their trips... with these special adventures in mind. Since you can only accomplish a limited amount of activities, sightseeing and attraction visits in any vacation or holiday trip, you will now have the ability to stay in locations for extended periods allowing for more in-depth coverage if you wish. More time to explore popular destinations and more time to experience the local scene in a destination you always dreamed about. This is how Workamping helps RVers experience the country one job at a time. The world is wide and the adventures are long- this is Workamping and you can go wherever the road leads!

What Can I Do?

The real question is what can't you do? And the answer is nothing! There is nothing you cannot do as a Workamper. Workampers have the freedom to choose jobs for short-term periods or for longer if they want, and they also choose the types of work they want for that particular arrangement. You can try popular positions like reservations and housekeeping or venture into more specific roles like activity and recreation planning. If you find the current position doesn't suit your skills or needs and wants for this point in your life, line up something different for future positions and keep going.

The most enjoyable Workamping comes into play when you are able to find jobs doing things you will enjoy and are at the very least comfortable with. It also happens when you are in a destination you enjoy and find interesting, as you will want to make plans during your free time to get out and explore locally.

I will say that the majority of businesses that currently advertise for Workamper positions are campgrounds and RV parks. But to be honest, I think this is because this is where the niche originated and these employers are more familiar with the term. We have seen a tremendous outreach from mainstream employers like Amazon, trying to find ways to incorporate their own seasonal workforce of RVers and I believe the need for such a reliable and well diverse employment pool is highly sought after. As more employers find ways to incorporate this community into their hiring and recruitment initiatives, we will continue to see the offerings for more and more mainstream or traditional jobs being advertised.

Outside the Box

Will you find other employers who are hiring RVers? Yes. Will you find employers who are looking for people to stay onsite? Yes. Will you find employers who offer onsite housing options such as cabins or mobile homes? Yes. And while all these job opportunities are essentially Workamping, they just have not yet accepted the term and as a result, miss the mark when trying to recruit. Don't let that stop or discourage you!

Workamping jobs and opportunities are all around us and all you have to do is dig them out! Look for employers advertising keywords in their ads and on the employment pages of their websites. If you're looking for a position at a ranch, search the page for the word 'ranch' and see what comes up. (On most computers this can be done by holding down the 'Control/Command' button and the 'F' key and then typing the word into the search field that pops up.) Also, it never hurts to think outside the box and reach out to a possible employer to inquire about the opportunity for setting something similar up with their business. You might snag a job for yourself and open their eyes to a whole new world of seasonal employees for future hires!

I know thinking outside the box is easier said than done for some people, but for those who are able to accept a less than traditional definition and refuse to put up defining walls or restrictions, they will be able to grasp the full spectrum of Workamping opportunities by keeping the options open.

Think about positions at retail stores, fulfillment centers, harvest fields, festivals, amusement parks, water parks, shooting ranges and more! All of these opportunities are open to those who have an adventurous spirit, a great attitude and the freedom to travel! Keep your mind open to all the possibilities that Workamping can open for you, and you'll do just fine!

How Much Can I Make?

I need to be as upfront as possible with you about the income you can expect from Workamping jobs. To be frank, it's not the best and it's definitely not the highest wages you'll likely have made in your life. But it is a modest reliable income that can help get you on the road faster than you thought possible.

A combination of paid positions, non-paid and volunteer positions as well as those that offer a combination, are what you will typically find from Workamping employers.

Many positions are noted for paying minimum wage or something slightly higher. These positions are the most common and include jobs that are easy to acquire and most anyone is capable of completing. They include things like reservations, housekeeping, landscaping, grounds crew, light maintenance, cash register operations, and check-ins. For these positions, you can expect to be paid close to the state minimum wage and should use your negotiation power when interviewing to assure you receive the best possible compensation plan you can.

Word to the wise: While I love to negotiate, it just doesn't work in every situation. I'll give you a heads up from one Workamper to another… negotiating with larger employers with well-established programs that typically hire hundreds of Workampers is a waste of time. Futile efforts my friends. Futile efforts!

3: *Understanding the Lifestyle*

As more and more people take to the streets and decide that traveling in an RV is what they truly desire to do, more and more people lack the basic understanding of the Workamping lifestyle. Workamping has grown tremendously in popularity and with that growth has come a new set of misconceptions, biases and new ideas as a whole. For instance, the idea that you have to be retired and living well off of savings income or monthly retirement checks has been debunked as more millennials and working-age RVers transition into the lifestyle. Other concerns about realistic living expenses, working for your site and being overqualified for basic jobs give new Workampers unnecessary worries before starting their big adventures!

Entering the world of Workamping can be a fun and exciting part of your life! I know when we first started we were filled with the joy of location freedom and the dreams of finding nooks and crannies across the map to explore with our kids. Workamping allowed us to pack up and go as we pleased. It allowed us to discover America on our own terms while making some income along the way. It can and will do the same for you if you understand first how it all works!

Making Sense of Dollars

Workamping is a niche lifestyle. It's an alternative way of living for some and a way to travel for others. For most folks, it is a combination of the two that seems to allow the best of both worlds. Workamping can be your ticket to travel when you have limited income from outside sources such as small businesses or hobbies that generate very little. It can allow you to take to the open road pre-retirement and stay afloat, so long as you are willing to make necessary adjustments to how much you pay out in respect to the income you have coming in.

Living in an RV can obviously lower your living expenses and free up cash to do fun things like exploring your new destination, but for some it can also provide the needed slack to pay off debt. Many people have found this to be true and continue to use it as such.

One thing that has remained the same if not pretty close to constant over the years, has been the cost associated with RVing. It's not free living!

It can be cheaper than a traditional travel lifestyle filled with hotels and even gives the American Dream of owning a home in the suburbs a run for its money, but let's be clear… it's not free living!

Many of the costs associated with RV travel can be greatly reduced and sometimes erased through the decision to Workamp along the way. Workamping lends its hand to help RVers save cash on things like housing expenses, site rental costs, paying for electricity at monthly sites, and having to pay for use of onsite amenities. Another huge savings is the fuel, as you will not be driving your RV daily from here to there, while Workamping. In fact, Workamping will allow you to stay for extended periods of time in some of the most desired locations in the US, where only local driving will be necessary.

Two Views of Workamping

Overall, Workamping was first and remains most commonly known as the optional travel life for adventurous souls who want to spend their days exploring and creating memories while staying active in communities across the US. In this view of the lifestyle, people choose to RV and live happy lives based around exploring new areas. They enjoy their days in short-term jobs that fuel their adventures and they use their off time to see and do as they please.

On the flip side, some have recently pegged Workamping as the fallback plan of those who fail to attain a standard of success and have no other choice but to wander aimlessly through life or what's left of it in search of low paying jobs as a migrant workforce. This was obviously not the intent of the Workamping lifestyle. The reality is that folks who have hit hardships have found that living the RV lifestyle, which offers reduce costs, is an attainable option.

You should choose which group you want to be associated with and what RVing will be for you.

Working for Site

A major consideration for people considering Workamping is "How many hours will I work for my site?" Personally, I like to respond with a big fat ZERO... but sometimes it's just not the case. Some employers will not provide a free campsite as part of your compensation and they will want a set number of hours worked to cover its cost. In this situation, since your job duties will depend on your position and the working environment may or may not be seen as an added benefit along with any other perks, you will need to compute how much you are being asked to pay for your site. Decide if the hours worked are benefitting you, the employer, or both.

Using this formula to compute the value will help you make sure the cost of the site is worth your time and energy:

Monthly Value ÷ Required Hours = Hourly Wage

Monthly Value: equal to the site rental fee (either based on the monthly or seasonal rate) + monthly utility cost + value of perks or additional benefits provided by employer.

Example:

> **Step 1:** $650 monthly site + $150 utilities + $100 perks = $900 monthly value.

> **Step 2:** $900 monthly value ÷ 80 hours (20 hours required per couple/per week) = $11.25 per hour

If this ever comes out to even a penny below the minimum wage, I would strongly suggest you rethink the decision to move forward with the job opportunity, unless there are huge benefits to being in that location during the specific time period the job would run. Also, if there is not a monthly rate available you should use the seasonal rate or something equivalent, but definitely not the daily rate by any means!

It's very typical now to see many jobs offering a site plus pay. These jobs will pay a general range of somewhere between $8.00-$12.00 per hour. If you can confirm a position with an employer who is paying $10.00 or more per hour and offers a FHU (full hook-up) campsite for FREE, you are doing well!

I don't say that to be cute, mean or funny… I say it because it is the absolute truth and I think you need to know this upfront. I want to help set realistic expectations and let you know from the start that you will not get rich Workamping! If making big bucks and living lavishly is your thing, this might not be the life for you!

Also, now is a good time for me to mention that depending solely on your income from Workamping jobs is not a good place to start. Not only have I been there and done it, but I did not enjoy it and it didn't last long. Workamping is much better lived with some other source of monetary funds flowing in. I like to think of it as a way to decrease costs and help pay the bills. It will not afford the luxuries of eating out, buying nice things, exploring the top tourist attractions, or even paying off pricey payment for big rigs with big notes.

Overqualified? Yes Indeed!

Workamping is not a career. You will not find career type wages in comfortable desk jobs with employee benefit plans offering a 401K and stock options, but it can still be a fulfilling way to earn some income while you travel! This lifestyle is typically centered around jobs in the outdoor hospitality industry and you should expect to be offered positions that involve interactions with the public as well as some based on basic computer skills.

It's easy to feel like your past experience in careers that may have dominated your previous life would deem you as overqualified for the majority of Workamping positions regularly advertised and you're probably right to feel this way! You are likely very over overqualified for 90% of the jobs you will be asked to complete, and this makes you the perfect choice for Workamping employers!

Workamping employers are tired of hiring from the local employment pool which includes people too close to home and those who may have just entered the workforce. They're looking for Workampers to diversify their team! They long for the chance to hire someone with a skill set they can depend on for knowledge as well as the professionalism that comes along with it.

Workampers looking to leave behind the pressures of working careers and fast-paced jobs are in luck. employers are looking for you! Include details about your field of expertise and areas where you have thrived in the past on your resume. If an employer is looking for someone who has electrical or sales skills, your resume will stand out if you are open to sharing this information!

Think it Through

Think thoroughly about how Workamping will fit into your life, or your new life as an RV traveler before you jump in. Hitting roadblocks are not fun when you don't have the time, patience or available resources to figure your way out. Do yourself a favor and get your house in order before you start this journey. You will be thankful that you did!

4: Knowing the Seasons

After a long winter, most likely in snowbird destinations like SoCal, the Arizona desert, Central & Southern Florida, and Southern Texas-Workampers are gearing up all across the country to make their way to their summer positions. Places like Yellowstone National Park, Camp Gulf, Adventureland, and a variety of private campgrounds in destinations many tourists can only dream about spending a whole summer, are gearing up to welcome new RV staffers.

It's one of the perks of the Workamping lifestyle- *freedom of location!* We choose where to go and for how long! Picking up a seasonal gig in that ultra-desirable tourist location and then spending the better part of the travel season getting to really know your surroundings, the community and having a blast exploring locally.

The Workamping Season

What exactly is the Workamping Season? Is it the same as the camping season? Do all Workamper employers hire for the same time frames? These are the questions that many ask time after time, as there has been some confusion on the definition of the actual Workamper Season... let's clear that up!

The official Workamping Season coincides with the camping season, which starts around Memorial Day and ends right after Labor Day. The exact dates are not defined nor are they important, because not only do employers hire for a variety of start and end dates, they also might ask you to start in the spring or stay through the winter.

During the Workamping Season jobs are plentiful. employers are also often overwhelmed with the response to their advertising and the interest to their open positions. Competition is higher overall, but can really be high for places like Alaska, Seattle, Maine, and National Parks.

Start applying early in the fall/winter and you will be successful in getting a head start on the masses. Line up your summer gigs before spring starts to make sure you get your perfect position. The Workamping Season is essentially the easiest time to find work. The winter, on the other hand, is more of a challenge, so let's spend most of our time in this chapter discussing those details.

The Winter Season

Family dinners, holiday parties, and for a lot of Workampers, the end of the Camperforce season all mark the start of the next leg of the Workamping adventure...the Winter Season.

Workamping during the winter really isn't unusual. It will require a little more planning and forethought than the typical route of securing a job for the Workamping Season!

The Winter Season brings a bucket load of questions, tons of uncertainty, and even some restlessness as the Workamper chooses to settle into monthly stays at snowbird-friendly parks in the south and far west, still wondering if they could have found a job for the winter instead.

The idea that Workamping during the winter is minimal - and to some extent none existent - is one to be taken lightly. It's pretty far from the truth if you're willing to step outside your comfort zones, plan ahead, and maybe use some creativity to find a position you feel good about.

Finding Winter Jobs

Finding a winter position might be a little easier than you think. Start with the basics on how you find work for the summer season, add some extra time and keep your eyes open for jobs when they first become available as well as those previously advertised.

My Top 3 Recommendations:

1. Use the information available. Check past and current ads as well as job alerts you may have received. employers purposely leave out dates to let working RVers know they have positions open during several times of the year. Sometimes you may have to jump out on a leap of faith by just sending your resume and letting them take it from there. It can't hurt!

2. Review past issues of Workamper News Magazine. Grab your stack of Workamper News Magazines and start flipping through the Help Wanted Ads section. Just because the ad was in a past issue doesn't mean the employer doesn't still have a need to fill that

position or others at their property. Check for ads that specifically say fall or winter as well as those without dates. Send your resume to the ones you're interested in as an attachment in a professional email.

3. Make sure to follow-up with each employer. Create a list of the companies you've sent your resume to for follow-up calls. I like to keep an Excel spreadsheet with columns *(employer name, 1st Email, Phone follow-up, 2nd Email, Offer, Confirmed, Notes)* to help me keep track and to help me remember who I've contacted, who replied, and what the next step is. When you're dealing with multiple employers you need to keep your information organized.

Can I Find a Job Right Now?

It's not a straight 'yes' or 'no'. There are many people who would swear that they found the perfect job at the very last minute and that their winter worked out great. But there are others whose story is the exact opposite, and you'll likely hear those stories first. So, I'll just say, there is a chance, but why not just plan ahead and be prepared? Planning ahead is going to be your best tool for success.

Workampers, especially those who wish to have the most desirable jobs during the winter, are known for booking jobs 1-3 seasons ahead to make sure they get the job they want the most. Be diligent and get a plan together of the next few seasons. Even a general idea of where you wish to travel will be a big help when you sit down to apply for open positions.

If you can't narrow down the exact location, try to plan what region of the country you'll travel to and look for a job in that area. If you find a great opportunity and are offered a job, base your travels around that location and enjoy what the area has to offer! The bottom line is, planning ahead will help you plan your adventure and make sure you don't always have to hustle at the end of the summer to find where you'll go next.

Avoiding Popular Destinations?

Florida, Texas, and Arizona definitely attract an insane amount of people in the winter, but don't let that scare you off - just think of it as another part of the adventure. And, if you plan ahead, you could be one of those super prepared Workampers who found a sweet gig camp hosting at a beachfront RV resort.

I personally love Florida, so I'd never recommend you stay away. It's an awesome state to live, camp, and work! There are so many attractions, natural and historical sites, beautiful coastlines, and tons of campgrounds to keep RVers as busy as they want, or not at all.

In the winter months while investigating opportunities in campgrounds, you will more often see compensation packages that just include RV site and perks. There are fewer offers of paying wages for extra hours or wages for all hours worked. This is likely due to the demand for these warmer locations that provide the employers with more bargaining power.

Many snowbird resorts are constantly full and taking a Workamping job in one of these resorts can help you get into an area you may otherwise have to wait years to experience.

A Few Tips

1. Look for year-round private campgrounds and RV parks.
2. Check into volunteer positions with state parks, U.S. Army Corps of Engineers projects, government-run operations, or non-profit organizations in states with warmer winter weather.
3. Contact Bowlin Travel Centers about positions in their stores and Dairy Queen restaurants in Arizona and New Mexico.
4. Research ski resorts who might need seasonal staff and shuttle drivers.
5. Consider positions that you can do anywhere! AGS, Southeast Publications, and Good Sam Travel Guide are three examples where you are selling ads and marketing packages all year long!

What Are Some Options?

Winter jobs exist at state parks, historical sites, private campgrounds, franchise parks, snowbird resorts, travel centers, ski resorts, retail stores, restaurants, and more.

These are all great options to get started with but don't limit yourself. You can find winter Workamping jobs scattered throughout the southern half of the United States and much of the West Coast. Options for Workamping during the winter can be endless, especially if you can consider options besides a traditional campground job.

The best part about Workamping is you can do just about anything. I know that sounds cliché, but it's true. Workamping doesn't have to just include campgrounds. You don't have to clean bathrooms, make reservations, or work in warehouses. You can do what you want. And as Workampers, we choose these jobs for one reason or another.

10 Ideas for Winter Workamping

1. House or property sitting
2. Sell something on Etsy, Amazon, or eBay
3. Work with an established company like All Pro Water Flow or NRVIA.org to start your own business helping fellow RVers
4. Sell photography to Shutterstock
5. Become a mobile RV technician and fix your neighbors' rigs
6. Sell some articles or blog posts
7. Start a dog walking service
8. Work for a credit card processing company.
9. Get involved with a direct sales distributor like Tupperware, Avon, Young Living, or doTerra
10. Earn affiliate commissions by signing up for a program like RVing Lifestyle Ambassadors

5: Resumes, Photos & Work Agreements

The top items on the recruitment agenda are resumes, photos, and work agreements. These three items are the topic of many conversations regarding recruiting Workampers and dealing with Workamper employers, so we need to discuss each one and get comfortable with the expectations!

An employer advertises your picture-perfect Workamping opportunity, which you are instantly excited about applying for... you then read that they are requiring a Workamper resume as well as photos of yourself and your RV. *What? Is that legal? Why do they need pictures?* Many questions start to cloud your judgment on if this is actually as great of an opportunity as you originally thought, and you take a step back to think for a moment. Before you write them off I urge you to learn more about the Workamper application process, how it differs from traditional hiring, and what is expected vs. required.

Let's start with Workamper Resumes!

Workamper Resumes

A Workamper resume is ideally a single page document that highlights your abilities and quickly details your past work experience. This can easily spread to 2 pages for a couple or family, which is totally fine!

Work experience should not be limited to what, if any, experience you have had in actual Workamping. You should also list past working experiences you've had in careers that will give you a leg up with employers looking for seasoned workers with specific skills.

When I created my Workamper resume, I didn't have any Workamping experience, so I could only include my past work experience, which I thought would be helpful to almost any employer! That included customer service, tons of computer and web skills, retail and sales experience as well as some event planning.

As I began to get job offers from employers who were in dire need of some 'new blood', I saw that not only were these offers being quoted at higher dollar amounts than what was being reported by fellow Workampers, but some employers were actually creating positions for me based on my experience and trying to bring a new surge of fresh energy to their businesses!

Don't discount your skills! List what you do best and trust that the perfect job opportunity will present itself! At the very least you've done your part by putting it out there. The ball is officially in their court.

Sending Photos

Many employers will ask for you to include a photo of yourself and your rig along with your resume. Many

Workampers are instantly put off by this practice and question if it's merely a method of discrimination for one reason or another. I have to say I both agree and disagree with the validity of sending pictures to employers. And while I have participated (in my own way) and encouraged the participation of this recruiting practice, it was for one reason and one reason only… to avoid myself or any fellow Workamper arriving at a job site only to be turned away.

With an ancient motorhome and 4 kids in tow, my husband and I never wanted to arrive at a new Workamper job with the employer not knowing exactly what they were getting. In the beginning, I would silently refuse to send photos, but would casually include a link to our blog with an invitation for the employer to get to know us… after 2 instances where the employer was shocked after arrival that we were so young and had multiple children, even though they still worked out well, I promised myself I would never drive anywhere until I had clearly laid out in an email with a time stamp, that we had 4 kids, this is what we look like, and this is what we camp in.

There is no way I wanted to drive any distance with the lingering fear of denial or rejection. When people ask me about why I think Workampers should just send the pictures, this is what I tell them.

Workamper employers are hiring you virtually. They are not taking the traditional interview route, which would require you to be present for at least one face-to-face interview. In return for not having to travel to their business for an in-person interview, which I was actually asked to do one time, do yourself a favor and send the photos or agree to a virtual interview over Skype or FaceTime!

Work Agreements

Once you have sent your resume, aced the interview and accepted the position, make sure your next step is to get everything in writing! When I say get it in writing, I don't mean a paper trail of email, although in a pinch this would work as well. I'm talking about a well-detailed work agreement that clearly lays out what is expected of you in your agreed upon position, what the hourly wage will be, how many hours, if any, will be required to pay for your site, among other things that are super important. You should have this document signed and in hand before raising your jacks to drive off!

Work agreements are not contracts, but they do serve as a common agreement between the employer and the Workamper on what was actually agreed upon. Sometimes you are hired months in advance, and even if that's not the case, sometimes people flat out forget all the details. Then it's simply the employer's word against yours and you might not feel comfortable approaching them about the differences once you've already arrived.

What to Include

- Employment start and end date, including how much time before and after employment you will be allowed to occupy the site.

- What type of RV site is provided for your use? FHU? W/E (water and electric)? Is the site included or do you have to pay for it? Can you pay in hours worked? If so how many per week/per person?

- Your position and the duties it requires. Don't assume that reservations won't include cleaning toilets... make sure you know ahead of time, what is required in the position you've chosen to accept.

- Will you be paid hourly? Is there a monthly stipend? Will the value of your RV site be reported on your W-2? Will a 1099 be issued? Is there a completion bonus? What is the overtime policy?

- What are the benefits other than monetary compensation that the employer is offering you? Wi-Fi? Propane? Golf cart? Free amenity usage? Onsite meals? Is there an employee discount? Does it apply to visiting family members and friends?

- Special Arrangements? If you've spoken with the employer specifically about a special arrangement like preset schedules or dates that you must have off, you will want to make sure these items are detailed in full on your work agreement as well!

In a perfect world, the employer would openly and graciously offer such an agreement to each and every Workamper they hired, but this world is far from perfect and that just doesn't happen! Some employers will be beyond prepared and have theirs sent over the moment you complete the interview, others will have you jump through virtual hoops to acquire one. You'll have to be persistent.

You will likely encounter both types of employers, although I hope you have far less of the latter. Make sure you do your due diligence in securing one for each position, and if you are unable- you'll have to decide if it's worth your time and trouble to make the trip without it.

6: Single & Solo Workampers

Workamping is the adventurous life of travel enjoyed by many Americans of all ages. Traveling from place to place, state to state, and job to job may not be a lifestyle made for everyone, but for many it affords the adventurous life they have always dreamed of while providing a modest income to boot.

Many of today's Workampers travel as couples, singles, and sometimes families with children in tow, sharing both the responsibilities of each new job and the lifestyle responsibilities of trip planning, driving, and the not-so-glamorous tasks included with setting up their campsite. But not all Workampers come in pairs, and for those who don't, there are often additional worries about finding employers who are willing to hire just one.

While these fears are not to be entirely disregarded, they are a little over exaggerated with the usually negative social media posts that dominate the scene.

Knowing the Difference

Let's first clarify the difference between a single Workamper and a solo Workamper…

> **Single** refers to a situation where one person is able/willing to work. This person may or may not be traveling with a partner.

Solo is describing someone who is traveling alone.

Many employers, in my experience, will try their best to fill spots with couples based on the simple fact that they can get two workers that only occupy one site. It's not personal, it's business. They're trying to lower their costs while being able to utilize the skills and labor force of two individuals compared to just one.

What you need to know is that employers are looking for both, those who can fill one spot and those who fill two. Solo & Single Workampers may not be the majority when it comes to folks who travel, but the reality is that many amazing people do this alone and their numbers are growing!

There are many employers who hire just one worker per site. Some employers only have one available position, or maybe they prefer to not have the possibility of personal issues trickling into the workplace and have made the choice to not hire those who live or travel together. Either way, it works in your favor. Embrace these jobs and these opportunities and you'll find there is a variety of options for you to choose from.

What Types of Jobs Are Available?

There are a variety of employers and income opportunities available for Solo & Single travelers. A mix of negotiation skills, creativity and patience is almost always a requirement.

30 Job Ideas For Single or Solo Workampers

1. Rides Operator
2. Lifeguard
3. Activity Director
4. Food Service Staff
5. Store Clerk
6. Campground Host
7. Raft Guide
8. Tour Guide
9. Docent
10. Groundskeeper
11. Security
12. Gas Line Inspector
13. RV Delivery Driver
14. Mystery Shopper
15. RV Inspector
16. Gate Guard/Attendant
17. Warehouse Worker
18. RV Tech
19. RV Detailing
20. Disaster Relief Worker
21. Shuttle Driver
22. Ski Instructor
23. Event/Fair Staff
24. Sporting Event Staff
25. Pet Grooming
26. Pet Walker/Sitter
27. Writer/Blogger
28. Photographer
29. Advertising Sales
30. Campground Map Sale

Who Hires Single & Solo Workampers?

Many employers hire one Workamper, some just don't make a point to directly state this in their recruiting ads. Others obviously love to recruit two strong workers to fill one RV site but welcome single workers with open arms if and when possible. Many employers would be in favor of one strong worker as compared to a couple where one half is seen as a thorn, so do your best to always inquire with employers about the availability for hiring one person.

In addition to many others, the following employers have said they specifically have positions for Single and Solo Workampers.

Various Locations:

- U.S. Army Corps of Engineers
- Texas Advertising - AGS Publishing
- Southeast Publications
- Express Employment Professionals
- Kitchen Craft
- Amazon Camperforce
- Bowlin Travel Centers
- Southern Cross Corp
- KOA: Kampground of America
- Equity Lifestyle Services/Thousand Trails
- RVing Lifestyle Network Ambassadors
- Sky Thunder Fireworks

State Specific Locations

- Xanterra Glacier National Park Lodges
- California Land Management
- Yogi Bear Camp Resort Wisconsin Dells
- Adventureland Amusement Park, Iowa
- Delaware North at Yellowstone
- Black Meadow Landing, California
- Greenlaw's RV & Tenting Park, Maine
- Yellowstone Silver Co., Montana
- Yellow Jacket Campground, Florida
- Lakeside Camp Park, Michigan
- Klink's Resort, Washington
- Vermilion Valley Resort, California
- Trinity Pines, Texas
- Indigo Bluffs RV Resort, Michigan
- The Cabins at Historic Columbine, Colorado
- Country Oaks Campground, New Jersey
- Cherry Hill Park, Maryland
- Black Bear Campground, New York
- Chocorua Camping Village, New Hampshire
- Three Rivers Resort, Colorado
- Mackinaw Mill Creek Camping, Michigan
- Pine River Lodge, Colorado

- Cottonwood Borco Ranch, South Dakota
- West Crooked Lake Resort, Minnesota
- Shenandoah Hills Campground, Virginia
- Spring Creek Campground, Montana
- Forest Recreation Mgmt., South Dakota
- Olis Trolley, Maine
- Jack's Campers, South Dakota
- Wall Drug Store, South Dakota
- Canyon Enterprises, Inc., Colorado
- Blue Bonnet RV Resort, Texas
- Okefenokee Swamp Park, Georgia
- Wilderness Aware Rafting, Colorado
- Rocky Mountain HI RV Park, Montana
- Partridge Hollow Campground, Massachusetts
- Treeland Resorts, Wisconsin
- Stonebridge RV Park, Texas
- Reelfoot National Wildlife Refuge, Tennessee
- Jekyll Island Campground, Georgia
- Sportsman's Supply Campground & Mountain Cabins, Colorado
- Sundance 1 Resorts, Arizona
- Corrington Enterprises, Alaska
- North Rim Country Store, Arizona

- YMCA of the Rockies, Colorado
- The Willamettans, Oregon
- Olive Branch Campground, Ohio
- Forever Resorts Parry Lodge, Utah
- Guadalupe-Blanco River Authority, Texas
- Taylor Park Trading Post, Colorado
- Detroit Greenfield RV Park, Michigan
- Idaho State Parks
- Glamis North Hot Springs Resort, California
- River View RV Park, Louisiana
- Cedar Pass Lodge, South Dakota
- Camp McPherson, Ohio

7: With Kids In Tow

Back in 2013 when we hit the road with 4 kids in tow to live a life of RV travel, let's just say it was not the norm. We were one of just a few families traveling full-time in RVs with the intention to work short-term jobs along the way. Family Workampers had not been heard of for the most part and we only met two others during the first year. But something changed between 2015 and 2016, as we approached another season at Amazon Camperforce in Campbellsville, Kentucky. When we arrived, we were met by an unexpected sweet surprise… families were everywhere, and it totally changed the experience for our kids and further normalized our decision to work and travel!

Over the past several years, we've met several families who travel and many others online that wish to travel in the near future. Most folks have a ton of questions and while some are specific to their life, the following are almost always asked about.

Can Both Parents Work?

Regardless of whether you need child care for younger children or not, both parents are able to work while traveling. This can be accomplished in a variety of ways and all revolve around what you find comfortable. For my husband and I, we choose to work opposite shifts, so we could easily work for the same employers. We would line up employment at various places and ask if one of us could work in the morning and then the other would work at night. We weren't particular about having the same off days, as we knew this would only be temporary, and to our surprise and enjoyment, it turned out to be a welcome change to those who wanted the same shifts. It always worked out for us!

A Few Things To Note:

1. A normal schedule included about 20-30 hours per person. We only worked 40 hours (or more) while working for Amazon Camperforce.
2. We made the most of our hours worked, by only accepting jobs where the site was offered for FREE.
3. Working opposite shifts gets old quickly. Not having the same off days as your partner in addition to starting your shift when they are ending their shift means you will not see each other very often.
4. Scheduling our stays at 4 months or less for these job locations made it more manageable.

How Much Will I Make?

I like to be very upfront and honest about this topic and may have said it before, but you will not get rich Workamping. You will make a decent wage and sometimes be provided a FREE site if you snagged a great position, but you will not be adding to your savings account or retirement fund by any means. If Workamping is your only means of income and you have kids in tow, money will be unreasonably tight, and the adventure will be overshadowed by financial woes. Do yourself a favor and find ways to earn extra income through a well-planned small business or income-producing hobby, also known as a side hustle.

What is a Side Hustle?

A side hustle is an additional income stream you can rely on for X amount of dollars. It's not your day job, a career or even your main Workamping gig- it's literally one or more things you've picked up for extra income on the side. In my opinion, everyone needs at least one side hustle, as multiple income streams are always best.

When we were Workamping, we also made money through freelance writing, affiliate sales from our blog, and little side jobs we picked up along the way from talking with fellow RVers, friends and family who needed services like content writing, proofreading, website creation, and email management among others. This also helped us not feel 100% dependent on working 40+ hours at every job. We could easily work 20-30 and have great adventures in our downtime!

Is It Harder Finding Jobs?

I can't say it's harder, because I never actually had a hard time. I can't say it's easy because it took a lot of well-crafted emails to get the jobs we wanted along with a great interview. Workamping with kids is different from those who do it without. So, you have to attack it differently and master how to pitch yourself to be successful.

For instance, when you see a job posted for a campground position you need to react a little quicker than usual. You don't have time to think about every detail. Give the employer a quick look, decide if it's something doable and then apply. You can do more research later, after your application or resume has been submitted.

In your email to the employer you'll need to craft a very polite and cheerful introduction including how you are excited about the possibility to join the team at a family friendly establishment, some details about the adults looking for work, maybe a recent accomplishment, and then mention you are part of a traveling family with x number of kids.

Let the employer know about your experience and why you'll be a great addition to the team. I usually added a sentence about how we did not need the same days off, but alternating shifts were preferable. Include pictures of yourself and the family as well as your RV or insert a link to your blog where they are welcome to go 'meet' your family.

Attach your resume with relevant work experience or just the previous positions that would highlight your skills. When it comes to family Workampers, I find it's better to show a severe over qualification, than to send too little information and hope they will ask the right questions.

Can Kids Come To Work?

This is such a tricky question and one that I think cannot just be left to common sense and good judgment. Bringing small kids or even younger teens into the workplace requires many things, but at least three to integrate seamlessly, which is usually just not the case.

1. You are assuming they will behave, be helpful and stay content throughout your shift without needing constant supervision or for you to hover over them.
2. Your employer, if they are okay with this, is assuming your children are well behaved (according to the employer's standards) and that they will not interfere with your work and in some cases may be able to help.
3. Everyone is assuming that the kids are aware of how to behave in the work environment, understand their role and the expectations set by you and your employer.

My husband and I worked as property managers for a resort and were faced with this issue more than once. We enjoyed a few well-planned days when our kids were able to come to work with us, which allowed for both of us to work at the same time. This amounted to my husband and I working with one of our twins by our side and our older girls split up with a park ranger to help with small tasks like refilling drink stations and golf cart patrol during school field trips on property. Easy Peasy! In this example, it worked well.

An example of it not working would be taking your kids to work with you when you are required to work on heavy machinery or in food service. Having your kids hang out with you in the office is also probably not ideal in the eyes of the employer or customers in person and on the phone.

So I guess it just really depends on what you're doing, where you're employed, and what the rules of the property are. Keep in mind it could also be doable on one day and then a totally unrealistic request on another.

I advise going into the situation with an open slate. If having the kids come to work with you is the only way to make it work, be upfront and honest with the employer from the beginning. You never want to travel any distance with the looming possibility that you may be turned away or asked to leave earlier than expected.

Are Extra Hours Required?

Occasionally an employer will come up with the 'great' idea that requiring extra hours for the kids or simply requiring hours based on the occupants of the site- regardless of age. I don't believe this is a reasonable requirement or expectation on behalf of the employer. If hours are being required to cover the cost of the site, which I seriously think you should try to negotiate to be completely FREE, you should not have to work extra hours to cover the kids' stay.

For example, I once applied to work at a family-friendly property in New York. During the second conversation with the owner of the property, I was told that 10 hours would be required for each person in the RV weekly. I laughed, thanked him for his time and moved on to my second option.

There was no way we were going to agree to work 60 hours each week just for the site. I found this to be an employer's kid tax initiative, which led me to believe his property was not as family friendly as he made it seem. I also use this judgment when traveling, for campgrounds who charge additional rates for children without amenities or anything more than a gravel parking spot.

I caution you against agreeing to such a situation, as you will not be getting a fair trade.

8: Top 7 Myths & Mistakes

With anything that involves a variety of people with a variety of opinions, Workamping is best known for some of the most inaccurate information! Preconceived notions about what it is and what it isn't are quickly followed by a host of common myths that are almost always trailed by a big mistake! In this chapter, we will dive into the top 7 Workamping myths and mistakes that you should know and avoid.

Myth #1: All Jobs Are Similar

Several types of Workamping jobs may seem similar on the surface. Working as a park host at one State Park over another may seem like a simple decision, but in fact, the two jobs can be uniquely different. Each job will have its own unique destination and that alone is worth doing research to look into whether the location is somewhere you want to spend a month, a season, or longer. Other differences can be the pay, job responsibilities, benefits, use of amenities and even the community or lack of one, regarding other Workampers on site.

Mistake #1: Taking the First Job Offered.

Once you've done all the planning and prep to actually make it possible to get on the road, you can easily lose yourself in taking the very first position that is offered to you. This is the biggest mistake a Workamper can make.

Not only are you literally not giving yourself a chance to grab the best possible position, but you're also probably not giving yourself time to think over the details of this specific job opportunity and what exactly it entails.

Do not take the first job you are offered. It is likely glowing and looks amazing simply because it's the first job being offered. Do yourself a favor and take some time, a day or more, to think it over completely. If the employer cannot wait for you to make sure this job is something you can wholeheartedly commit to, then this employer is not someone who you will want to work for.

Myth #2: Free = Trade For Hours Worked

Some Workamper employers will ask for a specific number of hours to cover your site rent. While this is a common practice, it is not the equivalent to providing a FHU. Working 20, 10 or even 2 hours to cover the cost of your site, is not free regardless of how you spin it. Make sure if you agree to work for your 'free site' that you calculate the number of hours you're working for it and see how much exactly you are being asked to pay.

Mistake #2: Pay Top Dollar For A Free Site.

Let's be very clear, a free site is one that costs you nothing and requires no hours worked in exchange. Working for your site or paying more than what a typical guest would be asked to pay is both wrong and underhanded on the part of the employer. Workampers should never have to pay a daily rate multiplied by 30 days in a month for their site. They should be provided a monthly or seasonal rate even if one is not publicly available. Workampers should also not be asked to trade more hours than would amount to the monthly or seasonal rate divided by their rate of pay, or minimum wage at the very least.

Since some employers are hiring Workampers to help the bottom line, they can sometimes forget entirely about how valuable your time and efforts are, not to mention the added bonus of hiring people who are skilled and have life experience. When accepting or reviewing positions, make sure you do your homework! Break out the calculator and put a dollar sign to your site to make sure it's free or at least fair.

Myth #3: Trust Every Ad

Employment ads for Workampers are no different from employment ads for other jobs, they are designed to highlight the good and reel you in as an applicant. employers are looking for people to fill positions and some will overextend themselves in an effort to do so (that's putting it nicely). Every ad you read is created to attract Workampers to apply and inquire further about the position. They should never be read as 'cut and dry'. These ads require further investigation to obtain pertinent details you will want to have before driving any distance!

Mistake #3: Not Doing Your Research.

You have to do your own research! Reading as many TripAdvisor reviews, blog posts, Workamper Experience posts as you can find, as well as doing a thorough read of the employer's website will give you a good overview of the business and possibly what it's like to visit and/or work at the location. You need this information to make your decision!

Now I know everyone has an opinion and that we don't always agree on things, but there is something to be said about hearing from past guests as well as past Workampers what you are getting into. You don't have to use this as your sole decision-making reference point but read through and have some information on the back burner for when you do!

Myth #4: Workamping Doesn't Pay

Many employers that hire Workampers are looking to get the most bang for their buck. As a result, they will advertise low wages for these jobs and some might even require more hours worked in exchange for a site than you are comfortable working. But this is not the case for all Workamper employers! In fact, there are more and more companies finding their groove in the world of Workamping and have found that compared to the local employment pool, Workampers are higher value even if you pay for all hours and give them a FREE site.

Mistake #4: Undervaluing Yourself.

Never underestimate the value of your contributions! Your time and your work are worth something, and they're likely worth way more than you think! Employers are thinking about themselves, for the most part, when they set their starting wages for new hires. You should do the same! Think about what you are bringing to the table and how you will contribute to the overall success of this business. Now do your homework and decide what your bottom dollar figure is and stick to it.

You should be able to negotiate at the very least the benefits that come along with the position you are accepting, if for some reason you are not able to get them to wiggle on the price per hour.

Myth #5: Multiple Seasons Are Best

Workampers might think that committing to multiple seasons with an employer is the best way to secure a position. While this is not entirely wrong, as many employers would love to hire for multiple seasons at one time, it isn't the only way to make sure you have jobs lined up for each season.

Mistake #5: Getting Stuck In A Travel Cycle.

Workamping is about travel and working along the way... You're not doing much travel and exploring if you continuously rotate between the same two or three jobs. I know this is super easy to plan and coordinate, especially with reliable jobs from big employers like Amazon, but it definitely leaves you stuck in a rut on a rotation that misses probably the best part of the lifestyle... freedom of location!

Before you schedule yourself for multiple seasons or multiple years at the same Workamping employer, consider venturing out and seeking something new. You might enjoy seeing different destinations and partaking in different aspects of Workamping. At the very least try not to repeat half of your jobs for any given year.

Myth #6: All Work & No Play

Repeatedly we hear someone in the crowd say "Workamping? I don't want to work!" And to be honest this probably is not the ticket to travel for them. Working along the way is one of the best ways to hit the road now! It is the single reason so many people in America have been able to travel full-time. Workamping involves work. Real work. It's a main component of the lifestyle that leads to other amazing benefits, such as the ability to travel!

Mistake #6: Not Taking Time To Explore.

Some folks do get caught up in the working part of Workamping. They find a job they enjoy and go hard at being the best. These are the Workampers that employers dream about. But sometimes these folks do not make time for exploring locally, which I feel is the biggest mistake!

We should all put our best foot forward and do so without hesitation wearing a big smile, but with work ethics in consideration remember why you started Workamping. For most of us, it will be for the adventures rather than the job. Make sure you don't just sleep on your days off! Take this time to get out into the surrounding area and explore! Find adventures both big and small around every corner and you will enjoy Workamping 110% more than you thought!

Myth #7: Apply, Interview & Done

I wish it were that simple! There is more to acquiring a good Workamping position than simply filling out an application and completing an interview. Some employers will want more than one interview, others will want to verify past employment and do background checks. Some will want pictures of you and your rig, others will ask for a virtual meet & greet. Workamping jobs are similar to those you've likely worked in the past, as in each employer will have his/her own way of doing things and you have to roll with it if you are serious about getting the job!

Mistake #7: Not Getting It In Writing.

A big mistake many Workampers both new and seasoned make is not getting a signed work agreement for each position they accept. Phone interviews and verbal agreements are great, but when you are traveling, sometimes thousands of miles, you want to make sure everyone is on the same page! There is no room for miscommunications and if you will go one step further and make sure you have all the details of your arrangement in writing, you can bet on a better experience every time.

Of course, I can't say for sure this will alleviate all chances of having an issue after arrival with what is expected vs. what was discussed, but having a signed agreement with what you've agreed to will help refresh anyone's mind who's confused, forgotten or dismissed certain details!

Start up a conversation at a campfire with a group of Workampers and you'll quickly find out Workamping is not for everyone. To be honest, it takes a special kind of person to enjoy the RV lifestyle in general, so once you add in the fact that you will be working along the way, well…. let's just say you're bound to find a soul or two that have had a less than desirable experience.

Use the information we just covered to help you avoid falling into this group of folks who have a salty aftertaste of the Workamping lifestyle and may have missed their chance to ever truly enjoy it!

9: Keys to Buying an RV

People spend months and even years dreaming about one day owning their very own RV to go Workamping. Packing up and taking off. Cruising the highways and byways of the good ol' U.S.A. and seeing all that this country has to offer is something special to look forward to. Regardless of whether your dream is living in an RV fulltime or taking the occasional Workamping road trip get-away, there are many ways to set yourself up to afford the price of owning an RV and making your dream your new reality.

One of the major reasons many people defer their dream of owning an RV is a false perception that they would not be able to afford one. Looking from the outside in, it often appears that only a small percentage of citizens have the financial ability and stability to afford purchasing and traveling in an RV. This couldn't be farther from the truth. To be honest, just about anyone can afford an RV and almost everyone can afford to travel in one.

There are four financial keys that you'll need to address in order to make your dream of living the RV lifestyle come true. I'm talking about establishing your purchasing power, earning income on the road, creating a working budget and last but definitely not least, decreasing your expenses. By addressing each key component, you can prepare yourself for the exact moment when your new reality will begin.

Establishing Your Purchase Power

For some people, saving is a top priority and for others...well it's just not a priority at all. But if you plan on making a big purchase like an RV, it needs to be your main priority. RVs are specialty vehicles - ones that come in all shapes and sizes. You first have to decide on what type of RV (Class A, Class B, or Class C motorhome, travel trailer, or fifth wheel) best suits your needs.

Then you'll need to think about what features you need. Do you need a king bed? Will you need slide outs? Each feature will have a price associated with it and you'll need to decide if it's actually worth the extra cost.

After you set your eyes on exactly what you would prefer to travel in, it's time to be realistic. Can you afford it? If so, great! But if not, you'll need to save aggressively and possibly make several compromises to make your dreams of living the RV lifestyle anything more than just sweet dreams.

Establishing your purchasing power is a combination of aggressive saving and research. How much can you save each month? What about each week? Set realistic goals and make yourself meet and exceed them.

Try reorganizing your income. Instead of paying your bills, buying food, clothing, and putting a little aside for savings; try putting your desired savings aside first, then allocate the remaining funds to your household expenses. You'll be pleasantly surprised how much you can save, by just adjusting the order you spend the money.

You also need to do your homework! Knowing the going rate for your chosen model of RV, what any upgrades are worth (both to you and in the market), are things that you need to consider before whipping out your checkbook.

After you've done your research and saved your coins, you are now armed and prepared to negotiate your way into the right price for your new RV!

Earn While You Travel

If you don't have a nest egg or retirement income that can sustain your travels, you'll definitely need to be creative when finding ways to make money while on the road.

Travel friendly jobs are the newest crave and lucky for you, there is almost something for everyone in this emerging genre. From online entrepreneurs and freelance writing and photography to traveling craftsmen, and of course Workamping jobs. There is definitely a full spectrum of employment opportunities where you can make a pretty decent amount of cash while traveling.

My first recommendation is to try to establish a source of reoccurring online income. Something you can do from your computer that will bring income into your bank account on a regular basis that only requires basic tasks like typing, uploading, and emailing.

Jobs such as being a travel writer will usually pay after publication, so money will continue to flow in as long as you continue to sell your work. Having a passive income like this, as the base for your travels, will make your adventure more financially stable and mentally comfortable by eliminating the stress of finding actual work while on the road. Second, I recommend booking some Workamping jobs with perks like free sites and utilities, plus hourly pay in a beautiful location.

Workamping can be a real life saver or budget saver for that matter! You can cut the expense of paying for your site by simply staying in areas for 3 months, or even a season, and earn a paycheck by doing jobs onsite that will further your camping knowledge and enjoyment.

Create a Travel Budget

You may be good at mental math, but this is no time to show off your skills. Everyone who travels, regardless of trip length, needs to establish a working travel budget. Not just a budget you made on your computer and never take the time to fill in either.

This budget will be your saving grace in times of despair and in times of enjoyment. It will tell you exactly how many more dinners you can afford, when to boondock when to change your oil, get new tires, and just how much you really spend on gas each month.

Knowing how much you have and allocating properly in the areas you need it the most, will make your trip more enjoyable by eliminating unnecessary stress. Your travel budget will undoubtedly be the most comprehensive document that you'll need to create before hitting the road. Every traveler's budget will include the following four categories. What you fill them with is entirely up to you.

Travel

Park fees, fuel, activities, and vehicle maintenance are just the tip of the iceberg when you start thinking of what your travel expenses might be.

Grab a sheet of paper and think of the items that you'll need to include to make your budget complete.

How many activities do you plan on doing in each place you visit? Are you staying in resorts or state parks? Is your RV covered for routine maintenance? How old are your tires? Will you try boondocking for most of the trip?

These are very important questions that you'll need to answer honestly if you want your budget to work.

Food

Everyone has to eat, right? Right. But what you eat and how much you spend on those meals is an entirely different story. Items like dining out, groceries, alcohol, and even specialty items like protein powder will need their own space on your budget if you plan on keeping track of what you're spending. Think about how you currently eat, and then think about what changes, if any, you'll need to make once you hit the road.

Personal Items

Personal items are where things can get a little tricky. Items like clothing, shoes and toiletries are expenses that almost everyone will need to budget for. But what about the extra things that make you smile - like entertainment or manicures? Did you budget for those things? If not, you'll need to add them to your budget quickly. It's really easy to overlook spontaneous expenses, so be sure to think hard when you're making your list and modify as things change.

Other

Insurance is the number one item in this category. In fact, you might choose to list insurance as its own category, depending on if you have several companies as providers or just one.

Memberships are also a big consideration. It's easy to get carried away with the number of membership accounts you have and how much you're spending on them monthly. Evaluate your membership accounts as they come up for renewal and weed out the ones that are no longer needed!

The last big consideration in this category is connectivity. Since you'll be spending more time on the road traveling in your RV, you'll need to make sure your phone and internet services are exactly what you need them to be.

Decreasing Expenses

After you've determined your expenses, it's time to focus on cutting back. Saving money each month by decreasing your expenses is a smart way to further your travels.

Reducing the amount of money paid out in various areas to far less than what your monthly income is will allow for extra funds to use on fun activities, rainy day funds, and emergency maintenance.

Many people assume, because RVers travel frequently, their expenses are high when actually it can be quite the opposite. Many RVers live comfortably on modest budgets while still enjoying what time on the road can offer.

Small modifications like these can be made to help decrease your expenses:

Cook your meals at home instead of dining out to save money on your meals. You can easily make enough for lunch the next day or two days of meals at once. You'll also skip the need to tip and can simply keep that 20% in your pocket.

Make an effort to travel at reduced speeds, maybe just 5 miles below the speed limit, to save on your fuel expenses. You'll add a few extra minutes to your commute, but the savings will add up quickly.

When reserving sites, make sure to search for spots with just the amenities you need. A heated pool is great, but why pay for it if you have no intention of using it!

As you can see, there are many ways you can prepare yourself to afford the RV lifestyle that you've been dreaming about. By starting with the four financial keys I've discussed, you can set yourself up for a successful start on your road to adventure.

10: Using Workamper.com

Workamper News is the #1 Resource for Workamping. They created the term and have championed its development for over 30+ years as the community has grown from humble beginnings to one of the most popular alternative lifestyles in the U.S. The main website workamper.com is home to an entire arsenal of resources for the active and soon-to-be active Workamper! This toolbox of jobs, media resources, and more has been known to be slightly overwhelming for those who are not comfortable navigating it.

Start at the Beginning

Starting from the beginning, which means creating either a free or paid account is your very first step. As a member of Workamper News, you are given behind the scenes access to the tools and information you seek. With this access, you can explore and research the lifestyle you are considering from the comfort of one complete and all-inclusive resource.

Without ever having to leave your account, you can read articles written by Workampers about topics ranging from tips on interviewing with employers and what a campsite is worth or how to know if you're being a pest or just persistent, along with information about campground reservation software. You can also browse the Media

Library which includes years, possibly even decades of material all relating to RVing. Some videos will walk you through complicated topics of RV maintenance and electrical issues, while others will provide you the basis for further exploration on topics pertaining to RV insurance, reservation software, live events, Workamping employer programs, and even Workamper training.

The Best Tools

Since there is so much to see and do on workamper.com, you may be wondering which are the best tools and resources that make purchasing the paid membership worthwhile. For those inquisitive folks, I direct your attention to the Awesome Applicants Resume Builder, The Real-Time Daily Hotline System, and the Workamper Experiences Database! These Top 3 Resources are what helps lead thousands of Workampers to find the perfect positions season after season and year after year!

Awesome Applicants Resume Builder

Many Workampers are often confused as to what information they should be providing to employers on their personal resumes. They are not sure if past experience in lifelong careers are considered valuable for positions that they are overqualified for. The answer is yes!

The resume builder provided as part of your paid membership will walk you through the minute details of telling your best story! It takes you by the hand and prompts you to fill out an extensive questionnaire form, that then generates a professional resume for employers to view and search through the system.

Providing additional information not typically found on traditional resumes like the geographical locations you desire to work in, when you are available, and even a place to add photos of yourself and your rig- make the Awesome Applicant Resume one of the most highly used and utilized recruiting strategies of Workamping employers who want to hire great people.

Sure, you could type up your old resume or just update a copy of your current one, but sometimes it's easiest to just use the systems that have been put in place to make it simple to get a successful final result. There is really no need to reinvent the wheel! And if you are in doubt, use both and extend your reach to employers.

The Real-Time Daily Hotline System

The Hotline system is the most sought-after tool of the Workamper membership, and for good reason! The Hotline Jobs System is made up of two parts: The Daily Email and the Hotline Jobs Page.

The Daily Email is sent out at 4 pm CST Monday-Friday and provides a detailed listing of all the jobs submitted for that day! Yes. You read that right… jobs submitted that day! That's huge! You are getting fresh jobs each and every day from employers who have a current need. They are actively seeking Workampers who are looking for jobs in great places and want to work!

The Hotline Jobs Page is a complete listing of all the jobs from the past 14 days. As jobs are sent out in the Hotline Email, they are then posted here for you to search and refer back to for the next 2 weeks, while they are considered active. The page allows for searching by keyword, published date, and location. You can also sort by date to see the newest jobs first.

While you may think you can find jobs on many FREE sites, you won't find many of these employers there! These employers have found the value in marketing their opportunities through Workamper News for the high quality of people they are able to find and hire repeatedly! You know the old saying "You get what you pay for!"

Workamper Experiences Database

If you are someone who thrives on understanding through reading reviews and experiences had by people who've been there and done that, then this is the tool for you.

Workamper Experiences, which was originally the Workamper Forums, hosts over a decade of information from fellow Workampers who want to help spread the word of both good and bad experiences. This is not social media. It's also not an employer bashing party. People are sharing real stories and real opinions that are aimed at helping fellow Workampers experience something great and wonderful or avoid something they felt was not well suited.

As a paid member of Workamper.com, you will have access to the complete Workamper Experiences Database where you can not only add employers and your personal feedback, but you can search and research future employers based on the feedback provided by your peers.

Always More to Come

This website is ever growing and always evolving to meet the needs and expectations of both Workampers and employers in the Workamping community. As the site continues to hold its place as the #1 Resource, where providing "Great Jobs For Great People In Great Places" is their motto, you can expect to have more in store as it gets bigger and better each and every year.

11: Finding the Jobs

By definition, Workamping is all about work and travel. Both pieces are equally important, but for some the work leads to the travel, thus making it a higher priority. Some people make a conscious choice to just work one season and use the remaining months of the year for exploration and personal adventures. Others will work season to season and find time to explore along the way and in the surrounding areas.

However you decide it's best to structure your Workamping lifestyle, make sure you know how to get the jobs that fit your needs and your wants. With so many different employers offering jobs to the RV community, sometimes it can be hard to figure out how to best go about applying for them, interviewing, and even negotiating the compensation you feel is appropriate for your time and skills. You can give yourself a leg up by knowing a few things before you make your first step towards obtaining these jobs. Let's take a look-

Be Prepared

Once you've made the decision to head out on the road, the only thing holding you back is finding that perfect job, right? To get the job, you have to be prepared with tools and information that will help you make the right impression from your first point of contact.

First, you'll want to know your personal boundaries. These are the things you will and will not do, what type of compensation you are looking for, and where you are willing to travel.

Armed with this information, you'll be able to negotiate your compensation with almost every employer you encounter. You will know what job duties you are comfortable doing and what things you just aren't willing to compromise on. For some people, this is cleaning toilets and for others, it's using a computer for reservations. Everyone is different, so choose your boundaries and stick to them.

Most employers will request a resume and having your outline of expectations will make it easy for you to create one. Don't be afraid to list your prior skills in lifelong careers, these skills are tried and true and you can use many of them in Workamping depending on what positions you are applying for.

Make a Connection

Think back to those corporate interviews - do you remember the type of questions they asked you? These are the same questions Workamper employers will ask you, so please be prepared.

When you apply to a position, do some research on the company. Pull up everything you can on their Workamper program and check out reviews posted by others who have worked for them. Give yourself a leg up by being prepared, then be ready for the interview where you'll need to connect with the employer to seal the deal.

Because you'll likely not be able to meet with the employer in-person, you will do all of your interviews with employers over the phone or via apps like Skype and FaceTime. Now is not the time to be shy or timid. Be you! Let your personality shine through.

Employers are looking for people who can communicate with them and form an instant bond. If you cannot connect with the employer over the phone, there is a really good chance you will not be called for a second interview and ultimately won't get the job. Your voice should show your personality and you should describe your skillset in a conversational tone without being pushy, brash, or interrupting.

Stand Out

Find a way to stand out! With thousands of other Workampers out there, the best tip anyone can give you is to find a way to set yourself apart from the masses.

What makes you the best bet for the employer? Why should they invest their time and money into training you to do a job with their company? What can you offer that sets you ahead of the competition?

These are the questions you need to have the answers to prior to applying for your first Workamping job. Think about these questions! Sit down and take some time to really plan out good answers that you can confidently convey to the employer during your interview!

Build a Network

There is something to be said about the ability to network in the RV community. Although many would disagree that it's necessary to get a job, I think we can all agree that having a solid network of contacts can make finding jobs easier by having one foot in the door!

I'm not saying that you have to be the social media king/queen and participate in every RV group discussion. But I am going to encourage you to get out of your comfort zone and talk to the interesting people you meet along the way! Building a network organically and naturally will serve you much better down the road than just inviting everyone to be your friend or follow you online!

Many Workampers attest to the ability to acquire their jobs just based on 'who you know'. If this is the case, it's better to play it safe and have a few contacts in your back pocket for a rainy day.

9 Steps to Getting a Job

Using the following steps will help you gain confidence in your Workamping job search. While each step is not necessarily hard to complete, they are each equally important and will take some time to accomplish. Researching employers isn't always the most fun task, but you will be glad you did.

- **Step 1: Pick a Location.**

Decide which states you want to work in for the period of time you want to work. If you have an idea of specific areas within the state, that's even better. Have a short list of at least 3-5 states to start, but please know the more options you give yourself, the better chances you have of finding work.

- **Step 2: Create a Resume.**

You will have to send a resume to apply for 99.9% of the jobs advertised, so you might as well get started. A Workamping resume is different from a general resume because it doesn't focus 100% on your past career experience, it focuses on your skills and the Workamping jobs you've had in the past. One resume is usually fine whether you are a couple, family, or solo.

- **Step 3: Apply ASAP!**

As soon as you see a new job posted, you need to apply! Do not wait until later. Do not wait until that night or that afternoon. Send them your resume right then. employers are bombarded with emails for these jobs, so the quicker you get your resume emailed, the higher up it will be in the stack. At some point they will stop looking at new resumes in their inbox; you need to make sure yours is already submitted by this point!

- **Step 4: Research the Employer**

It's easy to read an attractive advertisement and instantly think that this is the job for you! But how much do you really know about this employer and this opportunity? Make sure you take some time to research the employer, read reviews about their Workamping program and their property in general. If guests can't stand to be there, chances are you won't be able to either! Do your homework!

- **Step 5: Wait 1-3 Days to Follow Up.**

If you think employers will email you back, you're about 50% right. But as you can see, the odds are pretty risky - don't take the chance. Follow up on each job you apply for within one to three days of sending your initial interest. Call (if they provided a phone number in their ad) or send a quick email to see if they are still accepting applications/resumes and if the position is still open. Let them know you are very interested in the position and would love the opportunity to set up an interview!

- **Step 6: Nail the Interview!**

You have one shot to get this right! When the employer asks, "Are you available for an interview at ___." Your answer should always be "Yes!" While this isn't always possible, do everything in your power to avoid saying no. You need to make it easy for them to choose you. Once on the phone, show your personality and talk about how your skills will help their business. Don't go overboard, but really sell yourself! The first interview is the most important as it will either lead to the next step or sometimes seal the deal right away.

- **Step 7: Negotiate.**

You don't have to say yes to the first thing they offer you. Know your worth and find a way to negotiate the things you want/need to be able to happily complete your commitment. If the pay is low, ask for something higher. If the perks are blah, see if you can get your site for free or have use of park amenities like a golf cart or kayak. Find things to negotiate to make it worth your while. You'll thank yourself later!

- **Step 8: Get It In Writing.**

The worst thing you can do is set up a great job and not get the details in writing. This is called a Work Agreement and you should try to get one for every job you accept. I recommend never traveling to a new job without a detailed description of your job duties, start/end dates, schedule, compensation, perks, and end-of-season information. Do yourself a favor and ask the employer to send you a Work Agreement clearly detailing these items, if nothing more than just for peace-of-mind. This is not a contract per se, but a tool you can use to help get things back on the right track if issues arise during the season.

- **Step 9: Confirm Before You Travel!**

Before you pack up and embark on your road trip to your new job, make sure you email or call the employer to confirm your date of arrival. Never assume that nothing has changed since your last conversation, especially if it was months ago. Confirm the details with your next employer within the same week you plan to travel.

Part 2: Ways of Workamping

There are many ways of Workamping and I'm sure you'll find your groove with at least a few programs that fit your needs and suit your travels.

So, forget about fixing your desired schedule to fit that of your current employer... forget about starting on a date that is determined and desired by someone other than yourself... forget about doing a job you don't really want to do for a wage that you really feel is unfair.

With positions, compensation, and employers just as flexible as your travels, finding a job that suits all your needs is completely within reach. In fact, it's more likely you'll have a harder time choosing which job to accept and which jobs to postpone until the next year.

Workamping employers have the flexibility to structure and create their Workamping programs as they see fit. Some will offer career type benefits with a 401K and health insurance others will stick to the norm and just provide an hourly wage and a free FHU (full hook-up). It's up to you to decide if their location, compensation and job opportunities are a good fit for your travels and lifestyle.

In this section, I'd like to take a detailed look into the programs of 12 popular ways to Workamp.

12: Camp & RV Park Jobs

Before you start searching for jobs, take a minute to learn the details of the most popular type of Workamping operation, typical compensation packages and popular positions available... I'm talking about RV parks & campgrounds!

Campground Types

Knowing the types of campgrounds & RV parks looking to hire Workampers is a must for anyone looking for work while traveling. There are many other types of businesses that hire Workampers too, but if working in a campground excites you, this will help narrow your search when looking for employment. Let's look at three types and discuss the general idea of each.

Multi-Park Corporations:

You're likely familiar with names like KOA, Equity Lifestyle Properties, Forever Resorts, and Jellystone Park, but others like Sky Valley Resorts and Cal-Am Resorts also fall into the multi-park category. These entities operate campgrounds in multiple states which provides Workampers with a "wherever you want to go next" kind of freedom.

Though some of these resorts may have individual owner-operators, there will still be corporate or franchise rules and regulations to follow.

Typically, working for one of these larger entities will include some paid hours instead of just working in trade for an RV site. Due to the size of some of these parks, many Workampers enjoy creating a community of like-minded co-workers with multiple Workampers being hired at each location and sometimes in the same positions.

Private Parks:

Many jobs are offered by private individuals who own a small business that benefit from hiring Workampers who can relate better to their guests than other local hires. Often with individually- owned or family-run operations, you will become "part of the family" during your season there.

Each owner will have their own unique way of running their business, which you may or may not agree with. Dealing with "small town politics" isn't for everyone, and you hopefully won't find it at every park, but if you can learn to work around those situations and maintain a positive attitude, then working for a private owner will open the flood gates with a steady stream of job opportunities.

Government-Run:

Workamping at one of the many government-run parks can offer the ability to see new and exciting parts of the country from an insider's perspective while being entrenched in the natural beauty of the great outdoors.

Living on-site in these more scenic parks is completely different from a quick weekend road trip, offering more time to explore the surrounding area. With these parks, you often can negotiate shorter-term commitments. This differs from most commercial campgrounds, which prefer you work for an entire summer or winter season.

Government entities post job listings for multiple positions and time frames via volunteer.gov, their own city, county or state's website, and on the Workamper website.

Examples of these kinds of parks are state parks, county parks, U.S. Army Corps of Engineer campgrounds, and U.S. Forest Service campgrounds. Workampers in these parks are considered "volunteers" since they are most often working a minimal number of hours for an RV site (which may or may not have full hookups). These entities rely on the volunteers to keep the facility open and running, so Workampers often feel a genuine appreciation for their work.

Compensation Packages

Knowing the different types of compensation offered will give you a better idea of which jobs you should apply to. If you know these three main types of compensations, you'll know how and where to start your negotiations.

Knowing what the offer means beforehand will make sure you understand the work agreement prior to accepting the job.

Work for Site:

Working for your RV site is a great option for someone with an additional stream of income. Many campgrounds offer these arrangements in hopes of finding Workampers who are not relying on a paycheck and come instead for the beautiful scenery or exciting locale, along with a few hours a week of busy work. employers will offer a job in exchange for your site by stating something similar to this: "FHU for 12 hours per week."

FHU + All Hours Paid:

Probably the most desirable Workamping agreement is one in which the employer will pay you for all hours worked at a specified rate PLUS include an RV site with hookups. An employment ad might say: "FHU provided plus $10.50/hour for all hours worked. 30 hours/week."

This is a very attractive deal for the Workamper, because all their living expenses would be included, and as a result, these jobs would typically be the first off the market. Make sure to apply early and put your best foot forward. They'll have many applicants to consider and you will likely have just one chance to pitch yourself!

Combination Package:

In some cases, the employer will agree to pay for all hours but requires you to pay a reduced rate for your site. Or they may require a set number of hours each week to cover the cost of the site and utilities. This compromise is considered a combination package. Either you get paid for all hours and you pay for your site, or you work for the site and get paid for the additional hours. An example of this compensation would be an ad reading: "FHU for 12 hours, all others paid at $9/hour".

Words of advice: Make sure you have a written agreement that states the actual number of hours you'll work after the site is "paid for," or you could end up just working for your site.

Campground Positions

Now you know what kinds of campgrounds and compensation packages are out there, but what jobs tend to be most available?

Popular Workamping positions are just a starting point for your RV travels. Work is available all across the map in just about every job category you can think of but looking at what's most commonly offered at campgrounds will give you an idea of what to expect for this type of operation in particular.

Campground Host:

Campground hosting is the most iconic Workamping job you can get. It was the original Workamper job and as more and more people entered the lifestyle, more and more employers, including private, state and national campgrounds have started to hire campground hosts for their properties!

The idea of living on-site while welcoming fellow campers, answering questions, escorting, and closing the park gates are some basic job functions and picture perfect for many folks living the RV life. Less strenuous labor requirements, the ability to (usually) work from your site, and the opportunity to return year after year make these positions highly sought after.

Front Desk/Office Staff:

Along with the comforts of working mostly indoors with air conditioning, the job of the front desk staff is quite appealing for those who know their way around the computer. Entering reservations, checking out customers on a POS system, answering phones and assisting with customer questions and requests are the main responsibilities for this position.

Standing on your feet with little movement can be a downside, but based on your property location, this might not be an issue. Many front desk associates have a background in customer service or retail that serves them well for these jobs. But, even a newbie to computer reservations can pick up most park software relatively quickly with the right amount of training and support.

Activity Director:

As the most organized person on the campground staff, the Activity Director has to be well equipped with a Plan A, B & C at all times. Responsible for recreation, events, activities and the overall fun-factor of the property, you have to know your property, plan accordingly, and make sure each activity or event is structured and staffed to ensure guests enjoy themselves.

A typical day can include hours of computer work, researching crafts and creating themed games, as well as training the recreation staff on how to properly conduct the activities and then, of course, actually overseeing the events throughout the property.

Housekeeping:

This is hands-down the hardest Workamping job on most properties. Housekeeping is one of those love-it-or-leave-it positions. If you love what you do and you're good at it, then you'll enjoy it. If you don't, then just leave it alone.

Cleaning cabins, washing laundry, keeping up the bath houses and the main buildings like the office and cafe is hard work. It's made even harder by the necessity to redo the work throughout the day because the spaces may be heavily utilized.

Maintenance:

This is one of those jobs that no matter how much you do and how many employees are working together, there will always be something else that pops up. The job of property maintenance is never ending.

From sun up to sun down, there are jobs in different areas that will require attention. Some will be more pressing than others, but all will need to be completed ASAP. Typical duties can range from cleaning fire rings, to mowing lawns, to installing electrical in new cabins over the winter. Based on your experience, certifications, level of comfort and expertise, taking a job in property maintenance can mean a lot of different things.

The Reality

Workamping jobs come in all shapes and sizes...just like the adventurous people who apply for them! They are easily customized to meet the needs of the masses, making them perfect for you, your neighbor and your friend down the road.

Now that you know the types of opportunities and popular compensation packages that are typical, your job search will run smoother by allowing you to negotiate and tailor each job offer to meet your own specific job, compensation and living requirements. It is in your best interest to negotiate each and every agreement with Workamper employers to make sure you are getting the best experience in return for your hard work and dedication.

13: The Sugar Beet Harvest

Sit around a warm campfire from Winter to late Fall with a group of fellow Workampers and you're bound to hear at least one story from an adventurous soul who worked the Sugar Beet Harvest last year. Listen to the energized rants about freezing temperatures, weather-based days off and the exhausting 12 hour shifts that seemed to never end! Then pay close attention to the climax as the story shifts to a tale of a once in a lifetime experience, the beautiful friendships that were made, and the greatest pay in the shortest amount of time for any Workamping job. Now sit back and relax as groups of fellow RVers chime in on how they plan to make the trip to North Dakota & Minnesota this year for the exact same thing!

Overview

The annual Workamper migration starts after the end of the Summer Camping season, when Labor Day celebrations are just dwindling down. Workampers who have hunkered down in the top tourist destinations of the year, now make their way South, heading for snowbird approved destinations for the Fall & Winter months ahead. The highways are packed with RVers heading south and far west, but many RVers have a different idea. Easy to spot, since they might seem to be headed in the wrong direction, as they steadily drive farther north with their hearts set on racking in big cash before calling it quits for the year! They've signed an agreement with Express Employment Professionals to work the Sugar Beet Harvest, what they call an Unbeatable Experience. Committed usually for the full month of October, give or take a few days depending on mother nature's plan for the weather that year, they stand to rack in about $2500 a piece for just 2 weeks of work.

The Sugar Beet Harvest is championed by a collective effort between Express Employment Professionals who hires for the nation's two largest sugar producers, American Crystal Sugars and Sidney Sugars. Together they actively hire more than 1500 employees to work the harvest each year at 42 receiving stations and 6 factories. Since the local unemployment rate is pretty much non-existent, meaning everyone who wants to work is already working, Workampers are seen by some as the reliable infantry of seasonal help for the booming 5-billion-dollar beet industry. "Workampers are the heartbeat of our operation!" says Express Employment Professions. In fact, if you're a numbers person, you might be surprised, or at least interested to know that a whopping 42% of these 1500+ positions are filled by Workampers each year!

Obviously, Americans love their sugar! And while working the Sugar Beet is a unique Workamping experience, the hiring team likes to be upfront and honest about the details of this opportunity to ensure that Workampers are making the best decision for their personal situations when deciding if this opportunity is right for them. In a recent online webinar with the Express Employment Team, they made it *crystal clear* that these positions and this experience "is not for everybody" so make sure you read on and do your due diligence to gather all the information before submitting your application for this year's harvest.

Available Positions

There are a variety of positions for folks interested in the Harvest! This year alone, they have 160 positions at their Montana location and almost 800 at the locations in the Red River Valley. With that said, many Workampers make this short commitment a reoccurring staple in their Workamping arsenal before hunkering down for the Winter, so almost 400 of those are already spoken for by the almost 50% of returning Workampers. The following is a list of 3 major hiring categories for the harvest-

Helper/Sample Taker:

These are the general job positions Workampers are being hired for. The majority of applicants will be hired for these jobs, as this is the only position Express Employment can guarantee placement in. Basic job responsibilities include collecting beet samples and assisting the Piler Operators in cleaning and maintaining the area. Helpers will also communicate with drivers to ensure safe and accurate unloading of the delivery trucks.

Quality Lab:

6 indoor positions are offered inside the Quality Lab, where samples are tested to determine the farmer's pay for their crops: Dock, Tare, Scale, Brei Belt, Brei Mixer & LDB Quality. While these positions are all indoors and only require 10-hour shifts, positions in the Quality Lab are very limited, still require constant standing and are a very important part of the harvest operation. Workampers who wish to secure these jobs, are urged to apply as early as possible.

Skilled Positions:

There are a limited amount of skilled labor positions available each year. These positions require past knowledge and operation skills of heavy equipment and applicants will be hand selected by American Sugars directly. Returning Workampers who have proven their reliability and great work ethic are more likely to be accepted into these positions after year 1 is complete. If you are interested in these positions, send your resume along with your online application and be prepared for an onsite 'audition' once you are in the area.

> **Piler Operator:** Maneuvers the piler control switches, orchestrates repair work, supervises and assists in the cleanup of daily operations.

> **Skid Steer Operator:** Places deep freeze pipes and helps clean and maintain the pile area.

Working Conditions

As you can probably image, the working conditions of the Sugar Beet Harvest will be drastically different from the cozy campground store you might have worked in last Summer. The luxury of sitting for hours on end, chatting with guests about the crowding at the pool and installation of the new sauna should not be compared to the sights and sounds of working the harvest, as this is not a job you accept based on the beautiful view from your campsite, the perks of using the employee golf carts or the ability to explore the local area for new experiences.

How Can I Prepare For This?

Working the Sugar Beet Harvest is a strenuous Workamping job that will require some preparation prior to your arrival. During the summer prior to your harvest experience, it is advisable to add daily exercises like jogging, swimming, yoga, Pilates, stretching, and/or light weight lifting to your health regimen. Preparing your body for physically demanding work can help lighten the harshness of the physicalities you'll experience after arrival.

Start by slowly implementing exercise into your daily habits and grow to include more over the full course of the summer. Even small efforts like walking your dog more often and for longer periods or riding a bike to the store instead of driving will pay off in the long run!

Things To Know Before You Go

- The Sugar Beet Harvest is relatively short, at just about 10-14 working days.

- The pay is good and starts at $13/hr. Increases are given to returning workers who come back for consecutive seasons and those in skilled labor positions.

- Shifts are long and span a full 12 hours in most cases, during which you will spend most of your time on your feet.

- Your campsite is provided FREE as part of your compensation package, and you will not receive a 1099 at the end of the year or see the value noted on your pay stubs.

- The first 8 hours of your shift are paid at the regular pay rate, while the last 4 are paid at time and a half.

- Saturdays are paid at time and a half and they offer Sundays at either time and a half or double time-depending on the location.

- Temperatures drop below freezing usually during the nights, so all employees will need to be prepared to work throughout their entire shift wearing the appropriate layered clothing.

- Operations can shut down on days when it's too hot, too cold or too wet.

- When you complete your agreed commitment, you will receive a 5% Harvest Completion Bonus as an extra thank you for your hard work and dedication to seeing the project through!

- Basic job requirements require that everyone must be able to lift a minimum of 25lbs.

Campground Information

Working with 32 Campgrounds in the region, part of your compensation will include your site. Once hired on, the HR Staff will make your reservations and take care of all the details including paying for the site. Scott from Express Employment Professionals advised that "Not all campgrounds are created equal. The sooner you get your application in, the better your chances of getting a spot at one of the nicer ones." Most of the Campgrounds they offer provide a full hook up. If you by chance get a campground without sewer they will offer a honey wagon service free of charge. Also, if the temperature drops and the campgrounds have to shut off the water at the campsite, which has only really happened during the very last part of October when the season stretched out, they would provide a water truck also free of charge to fill your tanks. Some campgrounds will have a campground host on site, but not all are able to offer this amenity.

Most of the campgrounds are located very near to towns with gas stations, groceries, laundromats and hardware stores. But heading to Walmart and other big box stores would require more driving and possibly a shutdown day for enough time and energy to make the trip. They ask that Workampers arrive with enough propane and food rations to allow for two full weeks of work without requiring an errand trip to go get more, just in case.

The farthest campground is about 28 miles away from the piling site, so make sure you have a reliable vehicle or transportation to get to and from work, as walking would not be an option. Most sites are said to be about a 10-minute commute to work, which isn't bad and for Workampers without a tow or in town vehicle, carpooling with friendly neighbors is always an option.

Clothing Recommendations

With the temperatures ranging between cool and windy to dropping below freezing especially during the nights, you have to anticipate the need to layer your clothing. I can't imagine anything worse than working a 12-hour shift feeling unprepared and uncomfortable in a miscalculated wardrobe choice I could have prevented. Plan to layer your clothing for all shifts! You can always take a layer off if you get hot but trying to find an extra sweater lying around in a pile of beets, I can only imagine would be quite difficult. Insulated gloves, multiple pairs of broken-in boots, a few insoles or heated liners, thermal underwear, snow pants, heavy jackets, face masks, beanies, and hoodies are all recommended essentials!

The consensus seems to be that you should make a big trip to the thrift store for clothing you don't expect to ever wear again! Apparently, the smell of Sugar Beets isn't all that great and once the dirt gets on you, its stuck!

Hiring Process

- Submit online or by paper application, which they will mail to you.

- They will contact you for more information and to discuss details to move forward.

- Contact from your point person every 30-45 days leading up to the harvest.

- Arrival dates and campground assignment will be given after July 4th

Contact Details

Web: www.sugarbeetharvest.com

Phone: (888) 791-6738

14: Amazon's Camperforce

Working for the online super giant is truly an experience that's hard to put into words. There are so many pieces to the story that need to be told and there is usually very little time to tell it. To be honest, working at Amazon can best be described as working for a well-oiled machine. I know that sounds cliché, but it's true. Everything from the moment you step inside the building is planned, timed, scheduled, organized and then constantly being tracked, measured and observed for ways to make it better and more efficient.

Working in one of their fulfillment centers, inside the Camperforce program, means working for one of the largest, if not the largest, online retailer in the World. You're on the inside and you'll soon see first-hand what happens after a customer makes a purchase from their computer screen. You're working day in and day out to fill orders not only for customers, but most likely for your family members as well. Time is everything and your 'numbers' will show how your performance rates against the typical Amazon employee.

A Typical Day

A typical day depends on which department you're working in, the number of orders to be filled and what shift you're working on. Generally, you'll clock in after entering the building and dropping off personal items in your locker.

Clocking in for the day is a sight to see! Employees line up at every time clock and wait patiently for the exact second when their shift begins. Then one by one they scan their badges and proceed to their start areas.

After arriving at your start-up area you will meet with your department heads at a start-up meeting, where basic stretching is completed while important information is relayed through your Manager. After setting off to your station, or if you're a Picker– wherever your scanner directs you, your day will progress until either a scheduled break, lunch or the end of your shift.

Throughout the day, there is limited time to socialize with fellow campers or employees (unless of course you're a Picker) but making time for a quick "How's it going?" will help you maintain your sanity after hours and hours of repetition and checking your productivity.

At the end of your shift, you'll again notice an extremely long line of campers and employees at each time clock. As they wait for the clock to tick– conversations about 'work' and 'numbers' fill the air until the exact moment their badges touch the scanner and they exit the building!

First Things First

For first time applicants the application and hiring process for the Camperforce program can be long, drawn out and filled with delayed responses. From the moment you submit your resume or online application, wheels will naturally begin moving in your head. You're ready to go! Right?

Well, not so fast. When they say Application Process, they really mean it.

I would allow at least a month lead time from start to finish, and more likely 2-3 months, but then again, some folks get hired in just a few weeks, so you never really know.

There are hundreds of applicants sending in their resumes and only a small on-site staff of HR personnel to sort through them all. Give them some time and just plan on waiting a few days between emails and sometimes even up to a week in-between step. They do an amazing job of getting pretty much everyone who wants to work placed into a position!

Application Process:

- Fill out the online application on the Amazon Camperforce website.

- Provide proof of education (transcripts/diploma/degree). You must be a High School Graduate or equivalent.

- Pass Background Test & Drug Screening

- Start Date Given, based on the date you stated you are available.

- Pre-Employment Paper Work: Forms, needing to be completed prior to your start date.

- Orientation: Orientation consists of a few hours of Amazon policies and protocols and can be followed by a few hours of training inside the fulfillment center, so wear sneakers!

Knowing What to Expect

Even if this is your first time, you really do need to know what to expect. You should know what you're signing up for. Reading every review available will give you information, both good and bad. Just try to keep an open mind and pull from each personal story whatever information is given about the job, the available positions, the workload, the schedules, typical days, location information, community details and the expectations for Camperforce Associates.

Take notes on what you've gathered and transform these notes into questions. Once you're called for your phone interview, make sure to refer to your questions for the information you need to know. You can also bring up any unanswered questions at orientation or in a quick email to the HR Staff at the site you've decided is best for you.

The first year I did Camperforce, I really did have a horrible time. I dreaded waking up at 5 a.m. every day to go to a job I chose, only to realize I didn't like it. I had no idea what working in a warehouse was like. I had never even seen a conveyor system and barely knew what a tote was. As I looked around at all the smiling campers having a great time, I couldn't figure out what I had done wrong! Then it hit me - this wasn't what I signed up for. I signed up to fill customer orders in a fulfillment center. This was not what I had in mind!

If you think about my first experience, you've probably already noticed - this wasn't Amazon's fault. It was actually my own. I hadn't asked many questions when I agreed to take the position. I was excited and let that excitement overtake my rationale to ask any probing questions. I had absolutely no warehouse experience, but I never once asked what a typical day inside the fulfillment center would entail.

Being Prepared

Going into this job with the notion that you'll just "wing it," is the worst mistake a Workamper could make. Showing up to a campground to work in the store or maybe reservations for the summer may be something to "just wing." However, signing up to work at Amazon during their Peak Season, when millions of holiday orders are being pumped out at the very last minute, is something you should prepare for.

When I left Camperforce in 2013, I swore up and down, I would never return. Then after about a year, I started thinking...maybe I should give it another chance. After all, my horrible experience was largely the effect of my own lack of preparation. If I knew what to expect, I could have prepared. And if I prepared, I would've had a really great time just like the other Workampers.

Working in a warehouse is mentally and physically draining, so preparing for your job with the Camperforce program will require exercise prior to your arrival. In the weeks and months prior to your start date, I recommend you slowly increase your physical activity level and try to walk as much and as often as possible. Training your body for long periods of movement and even just standing for extended periods of time will help you adjust easier to life inside the fulfillment center.

In addition to physical labor, mental stamina will also be a major factor since employee safety is such a major concern. There are procedures and required protocols for just about every action you make and every job you will perform. You need to be constantly aware of your surroundings, as well as your own actions to make sure you're upholding the high level of safety Amazon expects at each of its locations. Preparing yourself both mentally and physically will make transitioning into your new role a whole lot smoother.

Top 3 Job Picks

There are three main positions that Amazon has been known to hire Workampers for over the years. These positions are responsible for, as Amazon Camperforce Representatives say, "Getting the right product, into the right box and shipped to the right customer, every time!" These positions are known as pick, pack and stow. Let's take a look!

Stow: (v) to put into a place for storage.

> Ex.) Employees will stow merchandise into their assigned bins within the fulfillment center.

When merchandise is received in the fulfillment center, the associates in the Stowing Department have the job of making sure it reaches the shelves not only in a timely manner, but also with the correct labels and into the correct bin so that Pickers can retrieve the items with relative ease. Stowers typically walk between 5-8 miles per day.

Pick: (v) to choose from a group.

> Ex.) Make sure to pick the exact item, as described on your scanner to avoid mistakes.

After products have been stowed properly, Pickers receive bin locations on their scanners, report to that location, and ultimately retrieve the correct product with 100% accuracy. The Picking Department is the largest department, involves the most walking (ranging between 8-12 miles per day) and makes up the majority of available jobs for Camperforce.

Pack: (v) to put into or arrange compactly.

> Ex.) Pack your items securely by using cello to fill your boxes before applying the label.

The Packing Department waits for the filled totes to arrive at their stations on conveyor belts. They then sort and pack the items into boxes to fulfill specific customer orders. Packing requires less walking than the above two departments, but physical activity is still required.

The Run Down

At the close of the traditional camping season, many RVers find themselves in search of a quick gig before heading south or west for the winter. Keeping everything, we've already discussed in mind, I consider working for Camperforce to be a great option for many Workampers including singles, couples, and even families. Amazon does a great job at accommodating all types of travelers, and with several positions, locations and schedules available, there's sure to be something that will suit your needs.

Who: Just about anyone and everyone can work the Camperforce program. People of all ages and backgrounds in all different rigs, campers and RVs. If you're relatively healthy, over the age of 18, able to pass a drug screening and background test and you have a 'recreation vehicle', you'll probably be hired. Check the website for exact details.

What: Camperforce is all about working in one of the nation's largest online retailer's warehouses. Amazon calls them fulfillment centers, but in an attempt to clarify, I'll make it clear– you will be working in an extremely large warehouse (possibly the size of a small village) with all the pros and cons that it entails.

Where: Camperforce is available at select fulfillment centers throughout the US. In 2015 there were four centers recruiting for the Peak season. Jeffersonville, IN, Campbellsville, KY, Murfreesboro, TN or Haslet, TX. Last time I spoke with a Camperforce representative, they were actively hiring for 6 locations all on the east coast. Check online for specific locations and to apply for these positions.

When: Typically, the Camperforce season starts sometime in early to mid-August running through Thanksgiving ending right before Christmas. Recently, the Camperforce program expanded their locations and the dates of the program, allowing for not only longer employment if desired, but also a range of dates and the ability to work at multiple sites back to back.

Why: Holiday orders of course! Camperforce is the brainchild that allows Amazon to keep up with supply and demand when it comes to pumping out millions of orders, usually in two days or less, while guaranteeing product accuracy and on time delivery.

How: An RV is your ticket to Camperforce. The program was designed for RVers looking for temporary employment while traveling in the United States. While campers come in all shapes and sizes, the bottom line is having one.

Last Words

While the program is open to hiring applicants of all ages and physical strengths, it is wise not to overestimate your own capabilities. These jobs are all very physical. Walking, standing for long periods, as well as lifting, bending and using multiple sets of stairs is required constantly throughout the day. Know your limits and make sure the job you sign up for is at a comfortable level within your physical ability.

Contact Details

Web: amazondelivers.jobs/about/camperforce

Phone: 855-9CAMPER

Email: CamperForce@amazon.com

15: US Army Corp of Engineers

The United States Army Corp of Engineers is responsible for almost 12 million acres of both land and water! It's a federal agency that maintains lakes, dams, marinas and campgrounds in various location in the US.

Not only does the Corp utilize volunteers and hire Workampers, but it does so at more than 400 projects offering opportunities for outdoor hospitality at recreation resources through what they call the Volunteer Clearinghouse and Contract Bids.

Volunteer Positions

As you know donating your time in return for perks like onsite living, flexible hours and less strenuous work requirements is quite appealing to many people entering the world of Workamping, as well as those who desire a more laid-back approach. Volunteering is also a great trial approach into the Workamping lifestyle as it allows for many to gain valuable work experience, references, and even launch several test trips prior to the actual commitment of diving in the deep end.

Although you are expected to serve without hourly pay, compensation for volunteer positions with USACE are often shorter in length, require less hours worked and come with a completely FREE site for the length of your agreed upon terms and as an added bonus, you actually receive the same benefits as federal employees since USACE is a federal employer- to my understanding.

What Can Volunteers Do?

At the Corps of Engineers, volunteers are utilized and needed in a variety of positions and roles. For those who appreciate natural settings and helping to maintain properties for public use, the Corps offers many positions in natural resource management as well as recreation.

While volunteering at the Corps, you may find more than one role where you are expected to help out and may fill in from time to time. As with many employers, hiring Workampers that are willing to be helpful and pitch in is a high priority.

The number one volunteer position is the Park Host, as you can imagine. The positions are very popular in the Workamping community and are highly sought after, making them pretty competitive. As a Host, you may be required to provide helpful information to the general public, greet visitors, answer questions, register campers, take reservations, answer the phone, open and close the park gate, as well as collect camping and day use fees.

While Camp Hosting may be the most popular, the following positions are also great opportunities inside the Corps parks to consider:

9 Positions Inside the Park

1. Trail Maintenance
2. Visitor Center Staff
3. Education Program Staff
4. Park Facilities Staff
5. Landscaping & Maintenance
6. Onsite Tour Guides
7. Water Safety Program Presenter
8. Beach Clean Up
9. Habitat Restoration

How Do I Apply?

If you are interested in volunteering with USACE, you'll have to get comfortable using the Volunteer Clearinghouse. This is a national information hub for all Corp projects which can be accessed either online at www.corpslakes.us/volunteer or by phone at -1-800-VOLUNTEER.

It's easy to apply and volunteer positions are always a great place to start for those who are new to Workamping as well as those who have just never worked with the Corp.

From the Volunteer Clearinghouse you will be able to find information regarding the specific opportunities currently available as well as the contact information of the Volunteer Coordinator or Park Ranger who you will need to contact.

Contract Positions

Different from the volunteer positions, USACE also encourages relationships with independent contractors for some of the day-to-day operations inside the parks. These contracts are provided by individuals for specific jobs such as Park Attendant, Maintenance, Mowing, and in some instances can be provided as a larger group in what is called an 'umbrella contract'.

Park Attendant Contracts

The Park Attendant is probably the most well-known, and possibly the most popular contract position with the Corp. In most situations, it will require 2 adults with no children under the age of 16, living onsite, providing the work needed to operate either a day use facility or campground.

The general agreement lasts between 4-7 months, usually in prime camping season, running from May-September and includes an RV site right by the entrance of the park. Working 8 hours per day for 5 days a week is a typical agreement. Evenings, weekends, holidays and even split shifts may be required.

Duties will vary by location and season, but most always include greeting visitors to the property and collecting fees. Additional responsibilities can include maintaining a record of sites, using the NRRS reservation system, answering questions, surveillance, opening and closing the front gates, light housekeeping, and enforcing the listed quiet hours.

How To Place Bids

As a general rule, contracts will be awarded to the lowest qualified bidder. If you've never bid on a government contract before, now is your chance to learn how! First things first, you'll need a copy of the contact specifications, that will list qualifications, deadlines, and procedures and bidding instructions. Contacting the Park directly or the District Office will point you in the right direction for how to proceed. Make sure to ask to be placed on the mailing list to receive an invitation for bids.

The amount you bid is entirely up to you, but make sure you've at least decided on your bottom dollar hourly rate. Multiplying this number by the total amount of hours in the contract requirements should give you an idea of what you are looking at for the season.

Either use this number as your base figure, onto which you will add additional monies, or simply bid with this figure.

USACE is a great option for those who enjoy outdoor recreation and hospitality. They are also known for having some of the most beautiful campgrounds with great options for recreational opportunities. You will find many contacts in part 3 of this book, whom you can contact with your questions regarding specific projects and positions.

16: California State Parks

Sharing your time in exchange for rewards, such as the opportunity to live in some of the most beautiful and sought-after locations in California from beaches to mountains and just about everywhere in between, is one of the main benefits of volunteering in one of California's State Parks.

A vital part to overall success of California State Parks, volunteers make up a large part of the staff. You'll notice them working tirelessly to educate and teach the public about these valued locations scattered throughout the state. The system's properties include more than just your typical idea of a state park. It also includes a variety of treasured resources like historic monuments, lighthouses, historic homes, ghost towns, beaches, museums, visitor centers, and even off-road vehicle parks. With over 40,000 volunteers to date who have contributed more than 1 million combined hours of dutiful service, the California State Park system which according to the California Department of Parks and Recreation, now includes "280 state park units, over 340 miles of coastline, 970 miles of lake and river frontage, 15,000 campsites, and 4,500 miles of trails", continues to thrive and grow.

"Working for California State Parks is more than just a job, it's an opportunity to become a steward of some of the most important historic, beautiful and culturally significant resources in the state," said California State Parks Director Lisa Mangat in a recent press release. "Our employees work tirelessly to preserve delicate environments, modernize visitor connections through technology, and protect and uphold the law – all the while remaining dedicated to living the parks life throughout California." *Living the Parks Life* is a phrase California State Parks uses to describe the life of those who work and volunteer inside the park system. They encourage people to "become a California State Parks volunteer and BE the difference!".

Why Volunteer?

Many Workampers are interested in volunteering for government agencies, charities and non-profits, where their hourly contribution is highly sought after. Their participation is heavily relied upon and the reward for such flows in forms other than monetary compensation. Volunteering can be a very rewarding choice for Workampers who desire experiences and benefits other than cash and have other means to sustain their travels such as savings, retirement or social security.

On the other hand, some folks have found that volunteering is an entrance ticket to paid positions or a way to gain experience in Workamping when they are just starting out. These folks accept a volunteer gig in hopes of gaining experience and building their Workamper resume to give them a leg up for future positions down the road. Overall, volunteering is just another way to Workamp. It's a way to travel and see the country in exchange for work completed at various sites along the way. I encourage you to think of the possibilities that working for an organization such as California State Parks would do, not only for you, but for the bigger goal of preserving and maintaining our country's natural resources.

As a volunteer you will have the opportunity to experience and learn history while living in a historical site and spending time in nature. You can help maintain and preserve the state's natural environment and help habitats that are endangered or in need of repair. Many volunteers choose to take on these opportunities for the chance of making new friends, meeting new people and sharing the things they learn with the general public.

What Are Some Positions That Are Available?

There are many positions available for interested volunteers to choose from! Your time and your skills will be contributing to maintaining the parks assets, encouraging visitor engagement, and sometimes behind the scenes tasks whose direct goals are to keep the parks operation up and running smoothly. You can volunteer as a campground host and live onsite at one of many properties, or maybe help out in the visitor center and conduct tours as a docent. There are also opportunities available for roles in maintenance, safety patrol, and many others!

Docents:

Becoming a trained volunteer historian who interprets the natural and cultural features of the state parks, is an amazing opportunity to have direct contact with park visitors. A highly trained position that requires continuous enrichment and training, Docents are able to receive the facts and information pertinent to the location, and add their personal style into the delivery. Job responsibilities may vary based on your location placement, but the opportunity to become involved with the educational programs, tours, living history reenactments and more, entice energetic folks to apply for these roles! People who are genuinely great with public speaking, have a knack for communications and a passion for sharing stories, are a great fit for these positions!

Public Safety Patrol:

The overall job of the Public Safety patrol volunteers is to provide safety information to the public. This includes; but is not limited to, first aid and emergency assistance that might be required during foot, boat, mountain bike, horseback or ATV patrol on property.

Park Hosts:

The most well-known job for a Workamper is a Park Host. The Park Host is the face of the park. A highly visible and accessible representative of the park system that assists day use and overnight visitors in a variety of ways from collecting fees, and cleaning facilities, to encouraging compliance with park rules and maybe even some light maintenance work. The

Park Host performs a broad range of job duties and is more like a jack of all trades than a master of one. These positions will usually require onsite living for ease of access and may require a 1-3-month commitment, or longer depending on the park. Some parks prefer long-term commitments, while other accept shorter stays from multiple hosts throughout the year. In most cases the park host will work about 20-30 hours per week in exchange for their campsite, utilities and access to the facilities. While many parks offer full hookups, there are some parks who offer a more rustic experience and have partial hookups or none at all.

Visitor Center:

If you're best at customer service, then the Visitor Center might be the best place for your service inside the park system! Every business needs a smiling cheerful and moreover, helpful representative to greet visitors and provide accurate information! You can be that person as a Visitor Center Volunteer! The main job duties will likely include answering questions in person and over the phone about the specific park amenities, trails, location and more, in addition to greeting guests onsite! Those who excel with direct contact with the public who also have great people skills and a friendly disposition should do well in these positions!

Natural Resource Protection:

These dedicated volunteers will play a critical role in the protection of natural resources in the California State Parks. Volunteers may be asked to assist with variety of hands-on jobs like exotic plant removal or relocations, trail maintenance and constructions, beach cleanups, habitat restorations and even native plant nurturing and enhancement projects. With something always on the list to do, to add to the overall welfare of the park, the Natural Resource Protection volunteer is a great position for someone who likes to stay busy and work with nature!

So How Do I Apply?

My suggestion before applying for any position is to thoroughly research the park, the location, and to find out the amenities that will be offered in exchange for your time. Since not all volunteer positions will likely come with the same benefits such as a campsite with full hookups, it's best to know up front what exactly you are applying for. Once you know for sure that the position is something you are interested in and capable of doing for the set time commitment, you'll want to complete a Volunteer in Parks Application.

Since each park is managed separately, you'll need to send your completed application to the volunteer coordinator at the park you are interested in working for. If applying to more than one location, be sure to send each location a separate copy of your application.

On your application, put your best foot forward! These positions will be competitive, and the best applicant will end up getting the job. Take your time to fill out the application entirely and to your best ability, paying particular attention to the education and employment background section and then attach a more detailed resume that further highlights your skills and experience! Make sure to provide the information for three verifiable references who can vouch for your work ethic and abilities as they pertain to these positions. The more information you provide to the volunteer coordinator the better chances you'll have.

Volunteer opportunities are open to those over the age of 18. A medical and/or criminal background check may be required, along with a State Park Volunteer Application and a Volunteer Service Agreement. Volunteers need to be both reliable and willing to complete assigned job duties, as like all Workamper employers, the state parks rely on you to help them during their busiest times and efforts are said to be made to match your interests, skills and desires to the positions available.

Contact Details

Web: www.livetheparkslife.com

Phone: (916) 653-9069

Email: Volunteer.inparksprogram@parks.ca.gov

17: Yellowstone National Park

RVers looking for adventurous summers in the nation's oldest and most sought-after National Park, are well served to spend their time working for Delaware North at one of several General Stores & Hotels inside Yellowstone National Park!

Imagine what a few months spent exploring natural wonders like Old Faithful Geyser, would be like! This could be the Workamping adventure you've always dreamed of, and its more attainable than you might think! As a Workamper in Yellowstone, you will have the ultimate 'local' experience of living inside the park and the spectacular ability to go beyond what millions of tourists are able to see in short visits and really dig in!

Delaware North

The National Park Service authorizes partners, such as Delaware North, to operate stores and hotels inside the park systems throughout the US. Delaware North operates about 300 stores in a variety of locations including Yellowstone, where 12 of its general stores are located along with three hotels in West Yellowstone.

As an employer, Delaware North does a great job to offer positions to a variety of people from all over the globe. From retirees to younger travelers, college students and everyone in-between, they hire a diverse group of people to help bring great experiences to visitors from all around the world!

Why Yellowstone?

When you make the decision to work at Yellowstone, you really make the decision to have a great summer! If you love the outdoors and/or have an urge to explore, this is the place for you!

Yellowstone is the place to be for the summer, regardless of your age! This is the cream of the crop when it comes to Workamping experiences because it offers so many activities for Workampers to enjoy throughout their time there. So, as you can imagine there are many reasons why you would want to apply for a position to work at Yellowstone with Delaware North. Let's look at some of them.

5 Reasons to Choose Yellowstone:

1. Yellowstone is the world's first National park.
2. With 1,000 miles of hiking trails, everyone can find their perfect hike from day trips to backcountry excursions.
3. Home to more than 10,000 geysers, hot springs and fumaroles to explore at your leisure!
4. Employee Recreation Program Co-op: Offers trips around the park for employees like rafting, sporting events, talent shows, backpacking and more, all for FREE.

5. 30% Employee discounts, with select 50% off days throughout the season!

The Yellowstone Workamping season usually starts early to mid-April and ends roughly at the end of November. Similar to Amazon Camperforce, you have the ability to provide a start date, and they will do their best to place you at one of their locations.

Expect to work 32-40 hours per week, per person. They hire singles, couples, and families, but make sure to discuss your scheduling needs up front. Sometimes split shifts are required which might not work for families needing opposite shifts to account for child care.

The team at Delaware North is very welcoming and do a great job of trying to accommodate everyone's needs. They also have a very straightforward approach to RV requirements... it just has to have all hard sides to be considered acceptable. Tents are not allowed.

Compensation

I'll cut straight to the chase, working at Yellowstone will not make you rich! The wages are on the lower side of the average and start at about $9.50 (sometimes more) an hour, paid weekly. But before you count it out, because you need to take into consideration where you are able to live for a few months... for that reason, I approach working at Yellowstone as a job you take to explore the location, not one that pays for further travel adventures down the road.

Also, as a huge bonus, like literally, you will receive a $3 per hour bonus for all hours worked on your final paycheck when you complete the time agreement you signed up for! That's a great bonus, when most employers offer $.50-$1.00 per hour bonuses!

Living At Yellowstone

Dormitories and RV sites are both available onsite living options for employees. RV campgrounds are shared with Xanterra employees but are not open to the public.

While FHU RV sites are not provided FREE with your employment, they are highly discounted and start at about $32 per week plus electric, which is payroll deductible. Most of the RV sites for Workampers are close to the stores, maybe a mile away, and if you are working at the Hotels, they are within walking distance.

Slides and size of the RV are some of the constraints of the available campgrounds. Sites that accommodate long rigs and those with ample space for slides will be limited, so try to plan and apply early.

To my understanding, Yellowstone is considered to be very remote. Big box retailers, hospitals and general shopping are not close by and would require a trip to town to pick up necessary supplies and medications, or to be seen by a physician.

Optional Meal Plan

A dining meal plan is available for about $64.00 per week, but only for the associates working inside Yellowstone. The meals are available 7 days a week and are payroll deductible, but you are only able to enroll and/or cancel this rotating menu one time during the season. Workers with strict dietary needs, as well as those working at the West Yellowstone location, may have to make other plans for meals. The meal plan is optional, except for those staying in the dorms.

Employee Health Program:

The seasonal employee health program known as Medcor, is not optional. Its required for all employees by the National Park Service and the cost is just under $8 per week.

Medcor isn't actual insurance or healthcare for that matter and should not be relied upon as such. It is more of a way to cover some of the costs of basic medical services offered at the three in park clinics, which are then offered at a discount to employees.

Limited Technology

It has been said that technology while living in Yellowstone is comparable to what was available more than a decade ago… this would obviously drive some folks crazy, while others will appreciate the chance to disconnect.

In some parts of the park the internet and cell phone connectivity are limited, and in others it's totally unavailable. Be prepared for this experience and think carefully on how being limited in your connectivity will affect you. Wi-Fi is available, though very limited, and some dorms have computers with internet available.

Verizon is the best cell provider in the park and pay phones are available at all locations.

Receiving Your Mail

Most of the locations have a seasonal post office for you to receive packages and mail. You can have your mail forwarded to these locations, but keep in mind, you will be unable to forward it back- so its suggested you stop the forwarding 2-3 weeks before your end date.

Available Positions

Most, if not all positions, are physically demanding and can be quite strenuous at altitudes between 6,000-8,000 feet.

- Inside the General Stores
- Cashier/Retail Assistant
- Cash Room Associate
- Stocker
- Warehouse Associate
- Employee Dining Room Cook
- Grill Cook
- Kitchen Assistant
- Custodian
- Inside the West Yellowstone Hotels
- Front Desk Clerk

- Host/Cashier
- Retail Clerk
- Housekeeper
- Laundry Attendant
- Line Cook
- Server/Bartender

Contact Details

Website: www.ygsjobs.com

Phone: 406-586-7593

Email: ygsjobs@delawarenorth.com

18: AGS Publications

Earn extra income as you travel with AGS Publications as part of their driving sales team for the campground industry. As one of the industry leaders in providing guest guides, campground maps, along with an array of digital marketing and web design services for campgrounds and RV resorts, AGS Publications has been in business for over 30 years since it was first founded in 1986.

AGS hires full-time RVers to join their team as Sales Representatives to sell advertising for guest guides that parks and campgrounds will then hand out to their guests upon arrival. If you've seen a guide in person, then you already know they are high-quality colored campground maps that also include pertinent traveler information like park rules, internet channels, dog walk locations, as well as a variety of local business options that travelers may find of interest.

Why AGS?

By representing a wide variety of privately owned campgrounds, RV resorts, as well as popular camping brands like KOA, Thousand Trails and Encore Resorts, the Sales Representatives at AGS Publications have the ability to crisscross the map from east to west and north to south as they travel and earn big commissions along the way!

Joining the ranks of the AGS Sales Representative Team allows you to define your travels from the very start. Unlike some other companies where leads are required, at AGS you are not alone in setting up your assignments. In fact, their home office handles this for you so you don't have to search for new assignments. Since you will typically only be working in 2-week increments, you can travel as much as you want, while bringing in a great income to boot. On your way from one assignment to the next, you can enjoy the freedom to stop and sightsee all the many things you've dreamed about when entering the RV lifestyle.

About the Job

Corporate training is provided to help ensure you are equipped with the knowledge you need to be successful and the tools you need to get the job done. Your training will last between 5-7 days and will be conducted by a corporate trainer, who is also a working representative. After successful completion, you will be given a number of assignments to begin immediately along with the confidence you need to hit the streets running.

Since your main job is to sell advertising to the local businesses surrounding the campgrounds and RV parks, you have the awesome benefit of staying in the park for 2 weeks, free of charge, while you scour the streets for sales! You will need to know your market of fellow RVers and be able to identify the local businesses that will most likely benefit from advertising to RVers. These businesses might

154

be RV specific or just traditional products and services they could find useful during their stay in the area.

The guest guides are provided to the business at no cost and are actually paid for through your advertising sales, which I would think makes for an easy sell!

You are only required to work 12-15 jobs per year but can request for additional assignments to make extra income if desired. Commissions are reported to reach as high as 70% of ads sold and are easily direct deposited into your bank account. You'll be happy to know they start from the very first sale! This is one job for RVers that allows for great income along with short stays and great travel opportunities!

Job Requirements

This is my own personal opinion, but I do believe you need a knack for sales, a generally friendly disposition and the ability to talk to people in depth about the benefits of purchasing these products to be successful. Sales are not for everyone, but for those who grasp how to do it and do it well, the opportunities are endless and the income can be huge!

AGS starts with an application that you can find on their website and then progresses applicants through a three-stage interview process. This method has allowed them to lead the pack with the lowest turnover in the industry by completing a full exchange of information and ideas. Their goal is to make sure there are no hidden surprises on either side once they bring in a new Sale Representative to join their growing team.

AGS Publications typically looks for applicants that meet the following criteria:

- Full-time RVers, with at least 6 months experience or several years of prior RVing.
- One team member needs a sales background.
- Willingness to work at least 12-15 two-week assignments per year.
- Must remain in contact with the office whenever an assignment is in production.
- Basic computer skills including email.
- Must be willing to attend the annual meeting every March to learn about new products & services.
- Flexible travels, as you must be open to go where the jobs are available.
- Must be driven and professional!

Contact Details

Website: https://www.agspub.com/rep-team-information/

Phone: 1-877-518-1989

Email: info@agspub.com

19: Adventureland Park

If you are looking to spend the summer some place where fun is plentiful, consider working at Adventureland Amusement Park.

In addition to the amusement park, Adventureland includes 200+ acres that also houses a 310-site campground and an almost 200 room hotel, just East of Des Moines in Altoona, IA right off exit I-80. A popular summer hangout, more than 600,000 guests are expected for the 2018 season!

Since Des Moines is just a short drive away, there is much to see and do in your leisure time while working inside the park. Workampers should consider using days off to visit place like the Botanical Center, Farmer's Markets, Blank Park Zoo, the State Capital, the Science Center and many other top attractions like the State Capital.

Working at Adventureland

The Adventureland Workamping program, which dates back many years of successfully hiring RVers, has become one of the most well-known summer Workamping jobs and for good reason. Adventureland Park has been hiring Workampers for many years and it's a well-known fact the current owner of Workamper News, Steve Anderson, was the original HR Director who initiated the program by bringing in thousands of helpful volunteers to add to the local hires.

Over the years, Workampers have returned to work for Adventureland year after year and many have brought friends and family back to join the fun experience. Throughout the season, they do a good job of encouraging employees to have a good time as well. It is reported that trips to local attractions, group games, ice cream socials, and other social activities are planned for employees to interact and have some summer fun.

Compensation includes a free FHU campsite during the season provided each Workamper is available to work up to 40 hours a week. Pay is calculated for all hours worked and starts around $8.50 per hour. Separate from other Workamping programs, they do not set time constraints on when your work agreement ends but do offer a seasonal bonus for those who stay through the end of the operational season. The end of season bonus is calculated at $.75 for every hour worked and an additional $400 campsite bonus is possible, if the majority of the occupants of a campsite are working during the season.

The current HR Director, Gary Pardekooper, has been known to start hiring right after Labor Day for the next season, but typically likes to wait until October 1. While the Workamping season at Adventureland runs from late April to late September, they seem to have flexible start dates with the caveat that all Workampers should be onsite by late June.

In April, at the beginning of the season, schedules will include part-time weekend hours only. Once the park opens for the summer and operations are in full swing, Workampers can expect to see daily full-time hours through the last weekend in September where 8 hours days, 5-6 days per week are normal.

Positions Available

Most positions will be inside the park facility in departments such as ride operations, retail, food service, and retail working 5-7 hour days with a 30-minute unpaid break.

Rides

Working in the rides department will include operating amusement park rides for park guests. Primary duties include assisting guests during the loading and unloading process and guest safety is a top priority. Standing on your feet for extended periods of time is typical in these roles, and they also require moderate lifting. You will be exposed to various weather conditions, so make sure you have appropriate gear.

Food Service

Food service employees are required to take and fill orders, operate the cash register, accept cash payments, and prepare some food items. Standing on your feet for extended periods of time is typical in these roles, and they also require moderate lifting when receiving and unpacking inventory. Safety is a top priority and requirements include use of (PPE) personal protective equipment.

Games

Inside the games department, Workampers can expect to work in many arcade/game areas throughout the park. Major responsibilities will include encouraging players to play games, handling cash payments, providing prizes to winners, and speaking over a microphone. Basic customer service and math skills are needed, along with an outgoing personality due to high guest interaction. Folks working in this department can expect to be exposed to various weather elements.

Retail

Retail Employees will enjoy working in one of several kiosks and/or souvenir shops throughout the park. Locations are located both indoors and outdoors, with varying weather elements. Job responsibilities might include tasks such as, using a register with point of sale computer, credit card processing, and stocking shelves. Employees in these roles should enjoy high customer interactions and be ready for a fast-paced work environment.

Dress Code

Adventureland has a dress code that is required for all employees. They will provide two work shirts, a sweatshirt and a raincoat. A $15 uniform deposit will be withheld from your first paycheck until the items are returned.

You are responsible for providing:

- Low cut black or white sneakers.
- A black belt, if wearing black shoes.
- A brown belt, if wearing white shoes.
- Khaki shorts, pants or capris.

Contact Details

Web: adventurelandresort.com/employment/workamper

Phone: 1-800-532-1286

Email: hr@adventurelandpark.com

20: Bowlin Travel Centers

Workamping opportunities inside the Bowlin Travel Center family means working at one of ten travel centers, five Dairy Queens, or Subway locations in Arizona and New Mexico.

Open 365 days a year, boasting long operating hours like 7am - 7pm, Bowlin is not your typical Workamping job. In fact, for some folks it's a Workamping career- that allows you to live onsite.

Working at Bowlin

Working at Bowlin includes customer service and sales. You will be working in a location that sells a combination of retail items, specialty gifts, gas, and food. These positions do not require experience beyond your typical customer service capabilities. The positions are hands on and require individuals who are self-motivated and enjoy public interaction.

Positions also require a variety of job responsibilities including the willingness to do everything from cleaning restrooms to daily paperwork. Doing whatever it takes to deliver a great customer experience is a top priority.

Bowlin employees usually work a 40-hour week. Hourly wages are paid in addition to a 5% commission for sales over a set threshold of about $50. While at work, Bowlin requires that employees cover all visible tattoos and that all piercings beyond one in each ear (for women only) be removed.

Positions

A variety of positions are available inside the Bowlin Brand depending on the location. Each location is different, and some will not offer all positions or possibly the same pay. Make a note to ask about availability at all open locations to make sure you are looking at the most attractive positions for that time.

Full Time & Part Time Positions Include:

- Manager-In-Training in Travel Center
- Manager-In-Training in Dairy Queen
- Customer Service/Sales
- Retail Clerks
- Maintenance/Custodial
- Inventory Specialist

Locations

All locations are located in either New Mexico or Arizona. Some are closer to the surrounding towns than others, and some can be downright remote.

I-10

- Akela Flats Travel Center
- Butterfield Stations & Dairy Queen

- Continental Divide Travel Center
- Old West Trading Post
- Picacho Peak Travel Center & Dairy Queen
- The Thing Travel Center & Dairy Queen

I-40

- Bluewater Outpost & Dairy Queen
- Flying C Ranch & Dairy Queen

US 70

- Running Indian at Alamogordo

Benefits

One of the best parts about working for Bowlin are the employee benefits. Unlike other Workamping employers, Bowlin offers a great compensation plan including pay for all hours worked, additional commission payouts, FREE on-site RV parking, 401k plan, paid vacations days, sick leave, bereavement and personal days, dental, vision and life insurance as well as uniform shirts and employee discounts!

Contact Details

Web: www.bowlintc.com

Phone: 888-240-7746

Email: humanresources@bowlintc.com

21: Kampgrounds of America

Kampgrounds of America, known as KOA to campers and travelers alike, has a unique Workamping program that stems from the ownership of more than 500 campgrounds throughout the United States. KOA developed its Workamper program with one extra special benefit... the ability to acquire travel vouchers for comped stays at KOA properties on your way to your next assignment!

Workamping at KOA

Hiring seasonal employees for predetermined time periods, KOA brings Workampers both retired and non, into their parks to help supplement their income while traveling in North America. Recently, KOA has seen a more diverse variety like many other Workamping employers of families with children and folks who are much younger than traditional RVers coming into their Workamping program.

Workampers are hired for a variety of job roles and commitment times, ranging from part-time and seasonal to full-time and year long. Most Workampers will be hired for about 6 months during the peak travel season depending on location and the park that you are interested in working at. Each campground will indicate how many hires they will need for any given time. Each park will also decide what the compensation will be for each position, although benefits like health insurance are never provided.

Typical Jobs

Based on the campground you are interested in working at, you'll have the opportunity to apply for a variety of typical campground positions ranging from Activity Directors and Reservations, to Housekeeping and Maintenance. If you are open to traveling to different areas of the country and keep an open mind on what positions are available during the season you are applying for, I would think finding a position with KOA would be towards the easy side of the spectrum. If it's a numbers game, which I believe it always is, then having the added bonus of applying for a position with a company with hundreds of site opportunities would lead one to believe the odds are in your favor.

Positions at KOA

- Park Management
- Front Desk Clerk/Retail
- Reservations/Office Staff
- Campground Host
- Activity Director
- Recreations Staff
- Site Escort
- Housekeeping
- Grounds Crew
- Landscaping
- Maintenance

Living On-Site

Although on-site living is sometimes required with the KOA Workamper program, almost all the KOA properties will require you to make arrangements for your own housing. This can either be living on-site in your own RV, living off-site in traditional housing, or living on-site in housing provided by the property. (If provided housing is something you are interested in, you will have the added responsibility of contacting the specific park and inquiring about the availability with them directly.)

Membership Required

Finding the jobs at KOA is a little different than finding your traditional Workamping jobs as they keep the majority of their posting on an internal membership site. To access the sites listings and information, you will have to purchase a yearly membership that costs about $35.

It should be noted that many parks still advertise their positions in traditional avenues for finding Workamping jobs like Workamper News, among others.

What's included in the membership?

- Access to KOA job postings
- Ability to post KOA resume
- *On the Road* e-newsletter for KOA Workampers
- Eligible for KOA Work Kamper of the Year award
- Travel vouchers to get from one job to the next!
- Referral rewards for recruiting friends
- KOA Workamper gift after finishing your first job.

Contact

Web: www.workatkoa.com

Email: welovekamping@koa.net

22: *Southern Cross*

Southern Cross is a Workamper employer who hires 'mobile leak survey technicians' that they kindly refer to as 'travelers' whose main job responsibility is to inspect gas lines to make sure they are working properly and then report the findings.

Natural gas lines have to be inspected regularly, that means every 5 years in most cases, but also every year for hospitals, schools, and business areas. As you can imagine, there is no shortage of work when it comes to identifying and ultimately preventing catastrophic situations. Most of the time the gas lines are said to be working as they should, but in the event where an issue is detected, your findings would be reported to the utility provider.

One assignment might have you assigned to a busy commercial district inside a metro area while the next would take you deep into a rural community where daily interaction with farm animals would not be uncommon. Talk about variety... RVers who are always up for new adventures and don't mind less than adventurous jobs to get them there will do just great in these positions.

Overview

A position with Southern Cross is not your typical Workamping job where you are on assignment for a specific amount of time then move on to another employer. In fact, it could be considered a mix of the best of both worlds since you work for one employer while traveling to new destinations with each new assignment. Both singles and couples are welcome to apply, but the one stipulation you should be aware of is that each person is treated like an individual employee. While couples would be placed on the same projects, transportation to work might get tricky trying to coordinate jobs in and around different areas.

Since they offer year-round employment, an RVer looking for a more permanent or reliable position without the need to line up gigs as they go, but still enjoy traveling to new cities both large and small might see this type of employment offer as a viable choice. At Southern Cross you would be given one job assignment at a time, for a specific amount of time, then move on to your next assignment in a new location without gaps in employment or benefits.

Each project is different. Some last from just a few weeks in small towns or rural areas, while others might extend for months in larger metropolitan areas. Assignments are said to never exceed 11 months. To my understanding, you would know up front what the time on each assignment would be as you are scheduled. They also make an effort to try to schedule travelers to an assignment for at least a month, so that you can negotiate a lower rental rate with the local campgrounds, which is an extra effort in my opinion to accommodate RVers and just a kind gesture on behalf of the employer.

Typical Day

Working for Southern Cross means working the hours of their clients on each project. That usually means 7am-3:30pm. In a perfect world, you would leave your RV campground in the morning and arrive at your assigned location at the designated time. Working at your own pace, you would walk over the buried gas lines (which are either under the sidewalks or slightly to the side) using your handheld instrument to 'sniff' the area for methane and check gas meters. Entering yards is typical to access the gas meters, which might require you to contact the homeowner to gain access if blocked or enclosed. Navigating according to the provided map, your day would continue until your day is complete and you return to your RV for the night.

Compensation

Personally, I think Southern Cross has one of the best compensation packages for Workampers. They hire employees, not independent contractors which means each traveler will have applicable taxes withheld from their hourly wages and they also offer benefits including health insurance, paid time off, paid holidays and 401K enrollment, which are hard to find from Workamping employers.

As if that wasn't enough, they also provide some really great perks for their employees which include covering some common living and travel related expenses, including mileage reimbursement and a per diem which are both not taxed.

Popular Benefits

- Starting hourly rate at $11.00/hr.
- $300.00 Per diem per week. (RV site and living expenses)
- Daily vehicle mileage is reimbursed at the IRS rate.
- RV reassignment mileage is reimbursed (when moving the RV from one project to the next). This reimbursement rate is .25 cents above the current IRS rate.

End of project bonuses are occasionally provided but should not be factored into anticipated earnings.

A Few Things to Know

- Survey technicians work outdoors in all weather conditions.
- They must be physically fit and able to walk 6-8 miles per day on varied terrain 8 hours per day, 5 days per week.
- Also requires the ability to be able to repeatedly lift their arms over their heads. Our first priority is the safety of our team, so we promote a culture of taking our time and staying safe.
- A large portion of the job is actually documenting our work on I-Pads, Android tablets and PC based laptops. Therefore, the ability to interact with technology is required.

- Map reading skills are a plus.

- Each technician must have viable transportation. This could be the tow vehicle (pick-up) or small car towed behind a motorhome.

- Every technician must have a valid driver's license and vehicle insurance.

- Travelers must find and secure their own RV park.

Contact Information

Web: www.southerncrossinc.com

Phone: 800-241-5057

Email: info@southerncrossinc.com

23: *Alaska Excursions*

What embodies the Workamper lifestyle more than great jobs in great places? A cool job in an awesome place, that's what! If you're looking into jobs that will provide adventures not only along the way, but also through your days, consider Alaska Excursions for a Workamping adventure to remember!

About AlaskaX

Alaska Excursions, or AlaskaX, is a newbie in the Workamper employer community. Their quickly growing tour company offers a wide variety of positions for Workampers looking to join their team in Skagway, Alaska for the summer. Skagway is a well-known, small town in southeast Alaska. Mild temperatures during the prime summer season make it an ultra-desirable location for outdoor enthusiasts and travelers alike. Hiking trails, gorgeous scenery and a variety of wildlife make taking a trip to Alaska for the summer an extra special bucket list item for many RVers!

Compensation:

As part of the AlaskaX team, you will be paid for all hours worked at an hourly rate of $12-$15 depending on your position. As an additional benefit, you will have the ability to experience all of their offered public tours for free as well as the ability to take advantage of other local tours for free or at a reduced rate.

Employee housing is available for staff members to rent in the town of Skagway. There is a free employee shuttle for those working outside the city with picks ups both to and from work locations. For those driving up in their RVs, AlaskaX has a private RV park located in town as well! Sites include water/sewer/electric and are available for $550 per month.

A typical season runs from the end of April to the end of September. If you can make the commitment to stay for the whole season, your application will be given preference over a partial season applicant, so keep that in mind when applying, just don't over extend yourself where you might have a problem completing your whole assignment. They do offer an end of the season bonus for employees based on completion of the season and a performance review. Staff members who complete their employment agreements and receive a positive review are eligible to earn a full bonus calculated at $2 per hour for each hour worked.

Working for AlaskaX

A typical day at AlaskaX is face paced with a lot of guest interaction! You can expect days lasting 8 hours on average in many positions and up to 9-11 for others. Your start and end times will vary by position, but in general will not be before 6:30am or after 8:00 pm. Overnights are also not a concern. Staffers can expect to work 4-5 days each week, leaving you some time to get out and explore the beautiful area and create some Alaska memories to take with you after the season!

Hiring both singles and couples, AlaskaX evaluates each applicant on an individual basis for the position they have applied. They do make an effort to accommodate both couples and friends with scheduling requests as often as possible. If you want same days off or opposite days off you will need to bring this scheduling concern to their attention early on in the hiring process.

Popular Positions

Providing the best possible guest experience with the greatest tour and excursions possible is one of their main goals, so being exceptional in customer services as well as a team player will be vital skills! Keep in mind that while they do accept applications for all positions and are happy to train the right individual, preference is given to applicants who have prior experience in the area they are applying. Also, AlaskaX utilizes Skype interviews so they can meet potential hires during the application process. These will be scheduled after your application is reviewed.

Adventure Guide:

Adventure Guides are tasked with the job of guiding guests on an adventure they will remember forever. Warmly greeting guests while safely driving and providing them with an entertaining tour along the way is a top priority. Guides usually stay with the guests all throughout the excursion entertaining them along the way and completing other tasks like picking up litter, cleaning guest bathrooms, and keeping the refreshment area stocked.

Office & Dock Staff:

Provide guests with their first impression either over the phone, through an email, or in person. The company's first point of contact for ship staff and other local companies, you will make sure all of the ships leave on time with the correct number of people on board. Making snacks and drinks for the different tours, selling tickets to prospective guests, handling guest reservations are all in a day's work! This position is great for people who thrive in fast-paced working environments, enjoy engaging with people and are always up for a new challenge.

Groundskeeper:

If you have a green thumb and a love of the outdoors, this position might be right for you! Your days will be spent brightening buildings with flowers and lush lawns, maintaining work spaces and natural trails. To excel in these positions, AlaskaX suggests staffers be physically fit and able to complete days of physically demanding repetitive motions and extensive walking in all types of weather.

Photographer:

Help capture guest excitement and experiences as part of the photography staff. Take pictures during excursions that are then provided for sale in the gift shop. Capturing the excitement of the moment is your main responsibility and being able to use creativity to precise timing will serve you well in these positions. This position is fast-paced and requires the skill to position photos for all types of weather.

Retail Sales Associate:

Assisting store customers in onsite gift shops also includes working in the coffee shop/bar and the photo sales department. Welcoming guests, answering questions, offering assistance, and handling cash/credit cards at the register are all daily tasks in this position.

Maintenance:

The maintenance staff performs a wide range of tasks throughout the company. These include, but are not limited to repairing, servicing, and building equipment of various sorts. They operate equipment such as loaders, excavators, dump trucks, and work vehicles. They even do things such as cut trees as well as build fences and cabins. They perform any task that is needed throughout the company.

Hiring Process

- Submit an online application.

- They will contact you for more information and to discuss details to move forward.
- Skype interview is scheduled.
- Employment decision generally made within a week.

Contact Details

Web: www.alaskaexcursions.com/employment

Email: Jobs@AlaskaX.com

Phone: (907) 209-6065

Part 3: Employer Information

The key to a successful Workamping lifestyle is having an arsenal of reliable employers and business opportunities! Regardless of if you intend to work seasonally, part-time or full-time you will need ample information on who is hiring, when they hire and what positions they usually have available. I suggest starting your own spreadsheet to keep track of this information and help you maintain necessary insight on specific employers for future reference. This can be as simple as just listing the employer name, contact information, and notes in 3 separate columns or as elaborate as you want with dates, pay and other information.

To help you get started I've provided employer information on over 1000 companies that hire RVers in this book! I haven't done all the work for you, but I've given the employer name and at least one piece of contact information to enable you to start your research. A word of caution: I've done my best to search for employers and information that made note of hiring RVers in some capacity. I did not contact each employer or contact listed for details or relevance. If you plan to reach out to these employers, it is my strong suggestion that you first look up their websites to find some general information. After you are confident in your findings and want to inquire about possible openings, you could then send an initial email with an introduction and inquiry for information and steps to move forward!

24: US Forest Service

The US Forest Service manages over 150 national forests and 20 grasslands in the US and Puerto Rico! Your experience can be put to good use by volunteering with the Forest Service in almost any position, outside of law enforcement and firefighting. As a volunteer, you will be one of over 2.8 million, since 1972, who have provided over 120 million hours of service!

While paid positions with the US Forest Service may also be available for seasonal or temporary jobs, which can be seen at https://www.fs.fed.us/working-with-us/jobs, as a volunteer you will also have the opportunity to earn an America the Beautiful National Parks & Federal Recreation Lands Pass for your service.

Make sure if you are interested in a volunteer position with the US Forest Service that you browse the open positions on Volunteer.gov and also contact the appropriate Program Specialist from the list below directly with your questions.

NATIONAL HEADQUARTERS

Washington, D.C.

- **Merlene Mazyck**
National Program Manager
mmazyck@fs.fed.us
- **Keyana Ellis Reynolds**
Program Coordinator

keyanaellis@fs.fed.us

NORTHERN REGION

Includes Montana, Idaho, North Dakota, South Dakota, and Washington.

- Joni Packard

406-329-3187

jpackard@fs.fed.us

ROCKY MOUNTAIN REGION

Colorado, Wyoming, South Dakota, Nebraska

- Kristin Schmitt

303-275-5384

kristinschmitt@fs.fed.us

SOUTHWESTERN REGION

Includes Arizona, New Mexico, Oklahoma and Texas

- Jennifer Nelson

505-842-3441

jennifernelson@fs.fed.us

INTERMOUNTAIN REGION

Includes Utah, Wyoming, Idaho, Nevada and California

- Bill Lyons

801-625-5458

blyons@fs.fed.us

PACIFIC SOUTHWEST REGION

Includes California and Hawaii

- Kathy Mick

707-562-8859
kmick@fs.fed.us

PACIFIC NORTHWEST REGION

Includes Washington and Oregon

- Emily Biesecker

503-808-2816
ebiesecker@fs.fed.us

SOUTHERN REGION

Includes Alabama, Arkansas, Florida, Georgia, Kentucky, Louisiana, Mississippi, North Carolina, Oklahoma, Puerto Rico, South Carolina, Tennessee, Texas, and Virginia

- Michelle Mitchell

404-347-1749
michellemitchell@fs.fed.us

SOUTHERN RESEARCH STATION

Includes Alabama, Arkansas, Florida, Georgia, Kentucky, Louisiana, Mississippi, North Carolina, Oklahoma, Puerto Rico, South Carolina, Tennessee, Texas, and Virginia

- Joyce Gorgas

828-257-4281
jgorgas@fs.fed.us

EASTERN REGION

Includes Connecticut, Delaware, Illinois, Indiana, Iowa, Maine, Maryland, Massachusetts, Michigan, Minnesota, Missouri, New Hampshire, New Jersey, New York, Ohio,

Pennsylvania, Rhode Island, Vermont, West Virginia, and Wisconsin

- Dawn Meier

715-362-1386

dmeier@fs.fed.us

ALASKA REGION

Includes Alaska

- George Schaaf

907-586-7876

gschaaf@fs.fed.us

25: State Parks

Included below is the best website address for seasonal employment and volunteer opportunities available for each state park volunteer system. This should serve as your starting point when searching for jobs inside the state park systems. If you have questions regarding specific positions or parks, contact that park individual to find out the most updated information on how to apply.

ALABAMA STATE PARKS

www.alapark.com/volunteering

ALASKA STATE PARKS

www.dnr.state.ak.us/parks/vip

ARIZONA STATE PARKS

www.azstateparks.com/employment

www.azstateparks.com/volunteer

ARKANSAS STATE PARKS

www.arkansasstateparks.com/about/employment

CALIFORNIA STATE PARKS

www.livetheparkslife.com

COLORADO STATE PARKS

www.cpw.state.co.us/aboutus/Pages/Jobs.aspx

CONNECTICUT STATE PARKS

www.ct.gov/deep/jobs

DELAWARE STATE PARKS

www.destateparks.com/Volunteer/VolunteerHosting

www.destateparks.com/GetInvolved/JoinOurStaff

FLORIDA STATE PARKS

www.floridastateparks.org/getinvolved/volunteer

GEORGIA STATE PARKS

http://explore.gastateparks.org/volunteer

www.gastateparks.org/ParkCareers

IDAHO STATE PARKS

www.parksandrecreation.idaho.gov/activities/volunteering

www.parksandrecreation.idaho.gov/seasonal-employment-idaho-state-parks-0

ILLINOIS STATE PARKS

www.dnr.illinois.gov/outreach/Volunteer

INDIANA STATE PARKS

www.in.gov/dnr/parklake/2443.htm

www.indianainnsjobs.com

www.in.gov/dnr/parklake/2439.htm

IOWA DEPARTMENT OF NATURAL RESOURCES

www.iowadnr.gov/About-DNR/Volunteer-Opportunities

KANSAS DEPARTMENT OF WILDLIFE & PARKS

https://ksoutdoors.com/KDWPT-Info/Jobs/Current-KDWPT-Employment-Opportunities/Volunteer-Opportunities

https://ksoutdoors.com/KDWPT-Info/Jobs/Current-KDWPT-Employment-Opportunities/Seasonal-and-Temporary-Positions

KENTUCKY DEPARTMENT OF PARKS

www.parks.ky.gov/volunteer/

LOUISIANA OFFICE OF STATE PARKS

www.crt.state.la.us/louisiana-state-parks/campground-host/index

www.crt.state.la.us/employment-opportunities/

MAINE STATE PARKS

www.maine.gov/dacf/parks/get_involved/volunteer.shtml

www.maine.gov/dacf/parks/get_involved/employment_opportunities.shtml

MARYLAND STATE PARKS

www.jobapscloud.com/MD/#EmpDiv55

www.dnr.maryland.gov/Pages/volunteer.aspx

MASSACHUSETTS DIVISION OF FORESTS & PARKS

www.mass.gov/service-details/learn-about-host-camping

www.mass.gov/service-details/volunteers-in-the-parks

MICHIGAN STATE PARKS

www.michigan.gov/dnr/

MINNESOTA DEPARTMENT OF NATURAL RESOURCES

www.dnr.state.mn.us/volunteering

www.dnr.state.mn.us/jobs

MISSISSIPPI STATE PARKS

www.mdwfp.com/museum/see-visit/volunteer/

MISSOURI DEPARTMENT OF NATURAL RESOURCES

www.mostateparks.com/page/55061/employment-opportunities

www.mostateparks.com/page/57872/volunteer-parks-program

MONTANA STATE PARKS

www.stateparks.mt.gov/volunteer/

NEBRASKA GAME & PARKS COMMISSION

www.outdoornebraska.gov/volunteer/

NEVADA STATE PARKS

http://parks.nv.gov/about/volunteer-and-support

http://parks.nv.gov/about/employment

NEW HAMPSHIRE STATE PARKS

www.nhstateparks.org/about-us/support/volunteer.aspx

www.nhstateparks.org/about-us/employment-opportunities.aspx

NEW JERSEY PARKS & FORESTRY

www.state.nj.us/dep/parksandforests/parks/volunteers.html

www.state.nj.us/dep/parksandforests/parks/jobs.html

NEW MEXICO STATE PARKS

http://www.emnrd.state.nm.us/SPD/Volunteering.html

NEW YORK STATE PARKS

https://parks.ny.gov/employment/

NORTH CAROLINA STATE PARKS

www.ncparks.gov/volunteer

www.ncparks.gov/Jobs/seasonal

NORTH DAKOTA PARKS & RECREATION DEPT.

http://www.parkrec.nd.gov/information/department/employment.html

OHIO STATE PARKS

http://ohiodnr.gov/contact/volunteer-with-odnr

OREGON PARKS & RECREATION DEPARTMENT

https://oregonstateparks.org/index.cfm?do=getinvolved.dsp_volunteer

PENNSYLVANIA STATE PARKS

www.dcnr.pa.gov/GetInvolved

RHODE ISLAND STATE PARKS

www.riparks.com/Employment.html

SOUTH CAROLINA STATE PARK SERVICE

www.scprt.com/state-park-service/volunteeropportunities

https://www.scprt.com/parks/jobs-at-state-parks/temporary-and-seasonal-employment

SOUTH DAKOTA PARKS & RECREATION

https://gfp.sd.gov/volunteer/

https://gfp.sd.gov/seasonal/

TENNESSEE STATE PARKS AND RECREATION

https://tnstateparks.com/get-involved/volunteering

TEXAS PARKS AND WILDLIFE

https://tpwd.texas.gov/state-parks/help-parks/
https://tpwd.texas.gov/jobs/state_parks/

UTAH PARKS AND RECREATION

https://stateparks.utah.gov/resources/volunteer/

https://naturalresources.utah.gov/seasonal-employment

VERMONT STATE PARKS

https://vtstateparks.com/employment.html

https://vtstateparks.com/volunteering.html

VIRGINIA STATE PARKS

http://www.dcr.virginia.gov/state-parks/camp-host

http://www.dcr.virginia.gov/jobs

WASHINGTON STATE PARKS

http://parks.state.wa.us/262/Volunteer-Program

http://parks.state.wa.us/774/Jobs

WISCONSIN STATE PARKS

https://www.dnr.state.wi.us/topic/parks/volunteer.html

WYOMING STATE PARKS AND HISTORIC SITES

http://wyoparks.state.wy.us/index.php/learn/volunteer-opportunities

26: Onsite Housing

If you haven't purchased an RV yet or you would just like an adventure that provides onsite housing options, the following list is provided for Employers who provide room and board for staff. You will need to verify if housing is provided free of charge or if fees are required. You might also want to verify the meal options available onsite as well.

DENALI PARK RESORTS

https://www.denaliparkvillage.com

YMCA OF THE ROCKIES

http://www.workintherockies.org

HOTEL IROQUOIS

http://www.iroquoishotel.com/

employment@iroquoishotel.com

ISLE ROYALE RESORTS, LLC

http://www.rockharborlodge.com

IDAHO ROCKY MOUNTAIN RANCH

http://www.idahorocky.com/employment/

info@idahorocky.com

FLATHEAD LAKE LODGE

http://www.flatheadlakelodge.com/

hr@flatheadlakelodge.com

ALTA PERUVIAN LODGE

http://www.altaperuvian.com/

THE LODGE AT BRYCE CANYON

http://www.brycecanyonforever.com/

SOMBRERO STABLES

www.sombrero.com/faqs/employment-with-sombrero/

jobs@sombrero.com

SIGNAL MOUNTAIN LODGE

http://www.workatsignal.com/

ADIRONDACK MOUNTAIN CLUB

http://www.adk.org/

jobs@adk.org

GRAND CANYON NORTH RIM

http://www.grandcanyonforever.com/

gnrhr@gcnr.com

ANDREW AIRWAYS

http://www.andrewairways.com

DEER VALLEY RESORT

http://deervalley.com/jobs

jobs@deervalley.com

KENAI FJORDS WILDERNESS LODGE

http://www.alaskacollection.com/corporate/careers/

HEART 6 RANCH

http://www.heartsix.com/

THE LODGES OF THE NORTHERN BIG HORN MOUNTAINS

http://lodgesofthenorthernbighornmountains.com/

CHISOS MOUNTAINS LODGE

http://chisosmountainslodge.com/

YELLOWSTONE FOREVER

https://www.yellowstone.org/

27: *Additional Employers*

Abiquiu Lake	austin.c.kuhlman@usace.army.mil
Alabama River Lake	kelli.m.little@usace.army.mil
Alabama River Lakes/Claiborne Lake	jason.r.swanner@usace.army.mil
Alafia River State Park	https://volunteers.floridastateparks.org
Alamo Lake State Park	bworman@azstateparks.gov
Alamo Rose RV Resort	https://www.rvresorts.com/alamo-rose.html
Alaskax	jobs@alaskax.com
Albee Creek Campground	blair.pubols@parks.ca.gov
Albeni Falls Dam/ Lake Pend Oreille	craig.s.brengle@usace.army.mil
Alfred B. Maclay Gardens State Park	https://volunteers.floridastateparks.org
Allatoona Lake	christopher.r.purvis@usace.army.mil
Allen David Broussard Catfish Creek Preserve State Park	https://volunteers.floridastateparks.org
Alta Lake State Park	volunteers@parks.wa.gov
Alum Creek Lake	robert.j.wattenschaidt@usace.army.mil
Amazon Camperforce	www.amazon.com/camperforce
Amelia Island State Park	https://volunteers.floridastateparks.org

American Land & Leisure	www.americanll.com
Anastasia State Park	https://volunteers.floridastateparks.org
Anclote Key Preserve State Park	https://volunteers.floridastateparks.org
Andersen's Oceanside Resort	http://andersensrv.com
Anderson Lake State Park	bill.drath@parks.wa.gov
Anderson's Landing	https://volunteers.floridastateparks.org
Andrew Molera State Park	sharon.pieniak@parks.ca.gov
Angel Island State Park	www.angelisland.com
Angeles National Forest	www.americanll.com
Anza-Borrego Desert State Park	norbert.ruhmke@parks.ca.gov
Aramark - Olympic National Park	http://www.olympicnationalparks.com/
Aramark Mesa Verde	http://www.visitmesaverde.com/
Aramark Tahoe Jobs	http://www.zephyrcove.com/
Arkabutla Lake	ernest.e.lentz@usace.army.mil
Arkansas River	michael.d.groves@usace.army.mil
Atchafalaya Basin Floodway	alison.k.hebert@usace.army.mil
Atlanta South RV Park	www.atlantasouthrvresort.com
Atlantic Ridge Preserve State Park	https://volunteers.floridastateparks.org
Atwood Lake	lydia.e.fach@usace.army.mil

202

Auburn State Recreation Area/Mineral Bar	asra@parks.ca.gov
Avalon State Park	https://volunteers.floridastateparks.org
B. Everett Jordan Dam & Lake	john.h.rochevot@usace.army.mil
Badlands Cedar Pass Lodge	http://cedarpasslodge.com/
Bahia Honda State Park	https://volunteers.floridastateparks.org
Bald Point State Park	https://volunteers.floridastateparks.org
Baldhill Dam /Lake Ashtabula	christopher.m.botz@usace.army.mil
Ball Mountain/Townshend Lake	dale.h.berkness@usace.army.mil
Bardwell Lake	justin.w.hebert@usace.army.mil
Barre Falls Dam	brianna.j.green@usace.army.mil
Barren River Lake	holly.l.myers@usace.army.mil
Battle Ground Lake State Park	volunteers@parks.wa.gov
Bay View State Park	volunteers@parks.wa.gov
Beach City Lake	lydia.e.fach@usace.army.mil
Bear Creek Lake State Park	vspvolunteer@dcr.virginia.gov
Beaver Lake	brian.walch@usace.army.mil
Beech Fork Lake	michael.d.mccomassll@usace.army.mil
Belfair State Park	volunteers@parks.wa.gov
Belle Isle State Park	vspvolunteer@dcr.virginia.gov
Belton/Stillhouse Hollow Lake	arthur.a.johnson@usace.army.mil

Benbow Lake State Recreation Area	christopher.glenn@parks.ca.gov
Benbrook Lake	lyndy.t.black@usace.army.mil
Benicia State Recreation Area	daniel.golde@parks.ca.gov
Berlin Lake	matthew.j.pook@usace.army.mil
Bethel Outdoor Adventures	info@betheloutdooradventures.com
Bidwell-Sacramento River State Park	matthew.stalter@parks.ca.gov
Big Basin State Park	www.bigbasintentcabins.com
Big Lagoon State Park	https://volunteers.floridastateparks.org
Big Shoals State Park	https://volunteers.floridastateparks.org
Big Talbot Island State Park	https://volunteers.floridastateparks.org
Bill Baggs Cape Florida State Park	https://volunteers.floridastateparks.org
Birch Bay State Park	volunteers@parks.wa.gov
Birch Hill Dam	jeffrey.c.mangum@usace.army.mil
Birch Lake	jeffery.a.walker@usace.army.mil
Black Butte Lake	amber.r.machado@usace.army.mil
Black Hawk Park	eric.m.hammer@usace.army.mil
Black Warrior/Tombigbee Lake	benjamin.h.sherrod@usace.army.mil
Blackwater River Heritage State Trail	https://volunteers.floridastateparks.org
Blackwater River State Park	https://volunteers.floridastateparks.org
Blake Island State Park	volunteers@parks.wa.gov

Blue Marsh Lake	nathan.t.freiwald@usace.army.mil
Blue Mountain Lake	jeremy.e.wells@usace.army.mil
Blue Spring State Park	https://volunteers.floridastateparks.org
Blue Springs Lake and Longview Lake	james.j.dickerson@usace.army.mil
Bluestone Lake	travis.d.daugherty@usace.army.mil
Bogachiel State Park	volunteers@parks.wa.gov
Bolivar Dam	lydia.e.fach@usace.army.mil
Bonnet Carre' Spillway	christopher.g.brantley@usace.army.mil
Bonneville Lock and Dam/Willamette Falls Locks	nicole.l.baker@usace.army.mil
Bothe-Napa Valley State Park	jason.jordon@countyofnapa.org
Bowlin Travel Centers	www.bowlintc.com
Boyce Thompson Arboretum State Park	bworman@azstateparks.gov
Brainard Lake Recreation Area	www.americanll.com
Brannan Island SRA	www.americanll.com
Bridgeport State Park	volunteers@parks.wa.gov
Bridle Trails State Park	volunteers@parks.wa.gov
Brooks Memorial State Park	volunteers@parks.wa.gov
Brookville Lake	stephanie.a.ison@usace.army.mil
Buckhorn Lake	priscilla.a.southwood@usace.army.mil
Buckskin Mountain State Park	bworman@azstateparks.gov

Buena Vista RV Resort	www.buenavistarvresort.com
Buffumville Lake/Hodges Village Dam	jamie.r.kordack@usace.army.mil
Building Pro	www.buildingpro.com
Bulow Creek State Park	https://volunteers.floridastateparks.org
Bulow Plantation Ruins Historic State Park	https://volunteers.floridastateparks.org
Burlington Campground	blair.pubols@parks.ca.gov
Burnsville Lake	ryan.s.davis@usace.army.mil
Butano State Park	shawn.wilson@parks.ca.gov
C.J. Brown Dam & Reservoir	brian.t.menker@usace.army.mil
Caesar Creek Lake	russell.r.curtis@usace.army.mil
Cagles Mill Lake	george.c(clark).baker@usace.army.mil
Cal-Am Resorts	http://www.cal-am.com/careers/
Caladesi Island State Park	https://volunteers.floridastateparks.org
Calaveras Big Trees State Park	barry.robertson@parks.ca.gov
California Land Management	www.clm-services.com
Cama Beach State Park	volunteers@parks.wa.gov
Camanche Recreation Company	www.camancherecreation.com
Camano Island State Park	volunteers@parks.wa.gov
Camp Gulf	www.campgulf.com

Camp Hatteras	camphatteras.com
Camp Helen State Park	https://volunteers.floridastateparks.org
Camp Wooten State Park	volunteers@parks.wa.gov
Canton Lake	shawna.m,.polen@usace.army.mil
Cantwell RV Park	cantwellrvpark.wordpress.com
Canyon Lake	samuell.h.price@usace.army.mil
Cape Cod Canal	elisa.d.carey@usace.army.mil
Cape Disappointment LCIC	volunteers@parks.wa.gov
Cape Disappointment State Park	volunteers@parks.wa.gov
Capps Crossing Campground	www.americanll.com
Carlyle Lake	kim.hammel@usace.army.mil
Carpinteria State Beach	cathleen.wills@parks.ca.gov
Carr Creek Lake	kevin.c.wright@usace.army.mil
Carters Lake	jonathan.r.wise@usace.army.mil
Castle Crags State Park	todd.barto@parks.ca.gov
Catalina State Park	bworman@azstateparks.gov
Cattail Cove State Park	bworman@azstateparks.gov
Cave Run Lake	anthony.w.orr@usace.army.mil
Cayo Costa State Park	https://volunteers.floridastateparks.org
Cecil M. Harden Lake	gary.j.staigl@usace.army.mil

Cedar Key Museum State Park	https://volunteers.floridastateparks.org
Cedar Key Scrub State Reserve	https://volunteers.floridastateparks.org
Center Hill Lake	sarah.j.peace@usace.army.mil
Charles Mill Lake	bryan.r.muroski@usace.army.mil
Charlotte Harbor Preserve State Park	https://volunteers.floridastateparks.org
Cheatham Lake	roger.d.austin@usace.army.mil
Chena River Lake (Chena Flood Control Project)	stewart.j.gilmore@usace.army.mil
Cherry Valley Campground	www.americanll.com
Chief Joseph Dam/Rufus Woods Lake	theresa.a.poulson@nws.usace.army.mil
China Flat Campground	www.americanll.com
Chippokes Plantation State Park	vspvolunteer@dcr.virginia.gov
Choice Hotels Gardiner, Montana	gm.mt411@choicehotels.com
Chouteau Lock & Dam	joshua.w.mathis@usace.army.mil
Christmas Decor Of Knoxville	http://christmasdecor.net/knoxville
Cider House Campground	www.ciderhousecampground.com
Circle K Guest Ranch	www.ckranch.com
Clair Tappaan Lodge	www.clairtappaanlodge.com

Clarence Cannon Dam and Mark Twain Lake	mary.a.heitmeyer@usace.army.mil
Claytor Lake State Park	vspvolunteer@dcr.virginia.gov
Clear Lake State Park	darin.conner@parks.ca.gov
Clearwater Lake	donald.henson@usace.army.mil
Clendening Lake, Piedmont Lake, Senecaville Lake, & Tappan Lake	lynette.m.christiansen@usace.army.mil
Clinton Lake	kipp.j.walters@usace.army.mil
Cochiti Lake	william.t.wallin@usace.army.mil
Cockroach Bay Preserve State Park	https://volunteers.floridastateparks.org
Coconino National Forest	www.coconinonationalforest.us
Cold Brook Lake/Cottonwood Springs	kody.l.green@usace.army.mil
Collier-Seminole State Park	https://volunteers.floridastateparks.org
Colorado Parks & Wildlife	www.cpw.state.co.us
Colt Creek State Park	https://volunteers.floridastateparks.org
Columbia Hills State Park	volunteers@parks.wa.gov
Columbia Plateau Trail State Park	volunteers@parks.wa.gov
Columbia State Park	volunteers@parks.wa.gov
Conchas Dam	ryan.j.poland@usace.army.mil
Conconully State Park	volunteers@parks.wa.gov

Conemaugh River Lake	april.l.richards@usace.army.mil
Constitution Convention Museum State Park	https://volunteers.floridastateparks.org
Cooper Dam/Jim Chapman Lake	dean.attaway@usace.army.mil
Copan Lake	matthew.k.schuffenhauer@usace.army.mil
Copano Bay RV Resort	www.copanobayrvresort.com
Coralville Lake	leah.c.deeds@usace.army.mil
Cordell Hull Lake	james.s.gregory@usace.army.mil
Corinth Recreation Area	www.americanll.com
Cottage Grove Lake	donna.r.bryant@usace.army.mil
Council Grove Lake	mieko.g.alley@usace.army.mil
Cove State Park	volunteers@parks.wa.gov
Cradle of Forestry IA	www.cfaia.org
Crater Lake Lodge - Xanterra	http://www.craterlakelodges.com/careers/
Crawford Caves	volunteers@parks.wa.gov
Crooked Creek Lake	karlee.l.kocon@usace.army.mil
Cross Lake Recreation Area	jason.a.hauser@usace.army.mil
Crystal Cove State Park	john.hunt@parks.ca.gov
Crystal Lake Family Campground	crystallakecamping.com
Crystal River Archaeological State Park	https://volunteers.floridastateparks.org
Crystal River Preserve State Park	https://volunteers.floridastateparks.org

Cuneo Creek Horse Camp	blair.pubols@parks.ca.gov
Curlew Lake State Park	volunteers@parks.wa.gov
Curry Hammock State Park	https://volunteers.floridastateparks.org
Custer State Park Regency Csp Ventures	jobs@custerresorts.com
Cuyamaca Rancho State Park	andrew.ferreira@parks.ca.gov
D.L. Bliss State Park	steven.oriol@parks.ca.gov
Dade Battlefield Historic State Park	https://volunteers.floridastateparks.org
Dagny Johnson Key Largo Hammock Botanical State Park	https://volunteers.floridastateparks.org
Dale Hollow Lake	bradley.potts@usace.army.mil
Dankworth Pond State Park	bworman@azstateparks.gov
Daroga State Park	volunteers@parks.wa.gov
De Leon Springs State Park	https://volunteers.floridastateparks.org
De Queen Lake	victor.r.kuykendall@usace.army.mil
Dead Horse Ranch State Park	bworman@azstateparks.gov
Death Valley Lodging Company	http://www.deathvalleyhotels.com/
Deception Pass State Park	volunteers@parks.wa.gov
Deception Pass State Park-Cornet Bay Fort Casey State Park	volunteers@parks.wa.gov

Deep Creek Tube Center & Campground	www.deepcreekcamping.com
Deer Creek Lake	bonnie.maki@usace.army.mil
Deer Lake State Park	https://volunteers.floridastateparks.org
Degray Lake	jeffrey.s.arthur@usace.army.mil
Delaware Lake	valerie.l.crane@usace.army.mil
Delnor-Wiggins Pass State Park	https://volunteers.floridastateparks.org
Devil's Millhopper Geological State Park	https://volunteers.floridastateparks.org
Dewey Lake	kayla.d.price@usace.army.mil
Diamond M Ranch	www.diamondmranchresort.com/
Diamond Valley Lake	www.dvmarina.com
Dierks Lake/Gillham Lake	trey.a.shelton@usace.army.mil
Dillon Lake	robert.w.cifranic@usace.army.mil
Dimond "O" Campground	www.americanll.com
Dollywood	https://www.dollywood.com/employment
Don Pedro Island State Park	https://volunteers.floridastateparks.org
Dorena Lake	donna.r.bryant@usace.army.mil
Dornan's In The Tetons	https://dornans.com/
Dosewallips State Park	volunteers@parks.wa.gov
Douthat State Park	vspvolunteer@dcr.virginia.gov
Dover Dam	lydia.e.fach@usace.army.mil

212

Dr. Julian G. Bruce St. George Island State Park	https://volunteers.floridastateparks.org
Drakesbad Guest Ranch	www.drakesbad.com
Driftwood RV Park	http://www.driftwood-rv.com
Dudley Farm Historic State Park	https://volunteers.floridastateparks.org
Dunns Creek State Park	https://volunteers.floridastateparks.org
Dworshak Dam	michelle.b.east@usace.army.mil
East Branch Clarion River Lake	arthur.myers@usace.army.mil
East Brimfield Lake	keith.w.beecher@usace.army.mil
East Lynn Lake	jason.a.kelly@usace.army.mil
Eastman Lake	kenneth.j.myers@usace.army.mil
Eau Galle Lake	william.k.schmidt@usace.army.mil
Econfina River State Park	https://volunteers.floridastateparks.org
Eden Gardens State Park	https://volunteers.floridastateparks.org
Edward Ball Wakulla Springs State Park	https://volunteers.floridastateparks.org
Egmont Key State Park	https://volunteers.floridastateparks.org
El Capitan State Beach	scott.anderson@parks.ca.gov
Eldorado National Forest	www.americanll.com
Ellie Schiller Homosassa Springs State Park	https://volunteers.floridastateparks.org

Emerald Bay State Park	steven.oriol@parks.ca.gov
Emma Wood State Beach	jeffrey.langley@parks.ca.gov
Enid Lake	kyle.c.tedford@usace.army.mil
Estero Bay Preserve State Park	https://volunteers.floridastateparks.org
Eufaula Lake	mark.f.limestall@usace.army.mil
Everglades National Park Boat Tours	http://evergladesnationalparkboattoursgulfcoast.com/
Fairy Stone State Park	vspvolunteer@dcr.virginia.gov
Fakahatchee Strand Preserve State Park	https://volunteers.floridastateparks.org
Fall River Lake	jesse.c.busenbarrick@usace.army.mil
Falling Waters State Park	https://volunteers.floridastateparks.org
Falls Lake/B. E. Jordan Lakes	stacee.l.henderson@usace.army.mil
Fanning Springs State Park	https://volunteers.floridastateparks.org
Fashoda Campground	www.americanll.com
Faver-Dykes State Park	https://volunteers.floridastateparks.org
Federation Forest State Park	volunteers@parks.wa.gov
Fern Ridge Lake	donna.r.bryant@usace.army.mil
Fernandina Plaza Historic State Park	https://volunteers.floridastateparks.org
Fields Spring State Park	volunteers@parks.wa.gov
First Landing State Park	vspvolunteer@dcr.virginia.gov

214

Fishtrap Lake	mark.r.holbrook@usace.army.mil
Flaming Geyser State Park	volunteers@parks.wa.gov
Florida Caverns State Park	https://volunteers.floridastateparks.org
Florida Keys Overseas Heritage State Trail	https://volunteers.floridastateparks.org
Folsom Lake State Recreation Area	flsra.camphost@parks.ca.gov
Fool Hollow Lake Recreation Area	bworman@azstateparks.gov
Forest Capital Museum State Park	https://volunteers.floridastateparks.org
Fort Casey State Park Fort	volunteers@parks.wa.gov
Fort Clinch State Park	https://volunteers.floridastateparks.org
Fort Cooper State Park	https://volunteers.floridastateparks.org
Fort Ebey State Park	volunteers@parks.wa.gov
Fort Flagler Anderson Lake	volunteers@parks.wa.gov
Fort Flagler Historical State Park	bill.drath@parks.wa.gov
Fort Flagler State Park	volunteers@parks.wa.gov
Fort Foster State Historic Site	https://volunteers.floridastateparks.org
Fort George Island Cultural State Park	https://volunteers.floridastateparks.org
Fort Gibson Lake	joshua.w.mathis@usace.army.mil
Fort Mose Historic State Park	https://volunteers.floridastateparks.org

Fort Peck Project	susan.e.dalbey@usace.army.mil
Fort Pierce Inlet State Park	https://volunteers.floridastateparks.org
Fort Randall Dam/Lake Francis Case	michael.d.insko@usace.army.mil
Fort Simcoe State Park	volunteers@parks.wa.gov
Fort Supply Lake/ Optima Lake	eric.r.summars@usace.army.mil
Fort Townsend State Park	volunteers@parks.wa.gov
Fort Worden State Park	fwv390@parks.wa.gov
Fort Worden State Park	volunteers@parks.wa.gov
Fort Zachary Taylor Historic State Park	https://volunteers.floridastateparks.org
Fountain Of Youth Spa Rv Resort	https://foyspa.com
Franklin Falls/Blackwater Dam	karen.w.hoey@usace.army.mil
Fred Gannon Rocky Bayou State Park	https://volunteers.floridastateparks.org
Frog City Rv Park	rvmanager@lafayettervpark.com
Gainesville To Hawthorne State Trail	https://volunteers.floridastateparks.org
Gamble Rogers Memorial State Recreation Area At Flagler Beach	https://volunteers.floridastateparks.org

Garrison Dam Project/Lake Sakakawea	eric.c.kelsey@usace.army.mil
Gasparilla Island State Park	https://volunteers.floridastateparks.org
Gavins Point Project/Lewis & Clark Lake	karla.j.zentenhors@usace.army.mil
Gaviota State Park	scott.anderson@parks.ca.gov
General James A. Van Fleet State Trail	https://volunteers.floridastateparks.org
George Crady Bridge Fishing Pier State Park	https://volunteers.floridastateparks.org
George W. Andrews Lake	joyce.s.sellers@usace.army.mil
Gerle Creek Campground	www.americanll.com
Gilchrist Blue Springs State Park	https://volunteers.floridastateparks.org
Ginkgo State Park	volunteers@parks.wa.gov
Glacier National Park	www.glacierjobs.com
Glacier Park Collection By Pursuit	https://www.glacierparkcollection.com/
Goldendale Observatory State Park	volunteers@parks.wa.gov
Grand Canyon North Rim	http://www.grandcanyonforever.com/
Grand Canyon South Rim	gcjobs@delawarenorth.com
Grand Teton Lodge Company	hr@gtlc.com

Granger Lake	amber.k.owen@usace.army.mil
Grapevine Lake	john.l.mathney@usace.army.mil
Grayland Beach State Park	volunteers@parks.wa.gov
Grayson Highlands State Park	vspvolunteer@dcr.virginia.gov
Grayson Lake	francis.s.jeffrey@usace.army.mil
Grayton Beach State Park	https://volunteers.floridastateparks.org
Green River Lake	jessica.l.lee@usace.army.mil
Greers Ferry Lake	joseph.d.harper@usace.army.mil
Grenada Lake	gaydon.w.clark@usace.army.mil
Grist Mill State Historic Park	jason.jordon@countyofnapa.org
Grizzly Creek Redwoods State Park	racheal.marte-taylor@parks.ca.gov
Grove River Ranch, Equestrian Center & Retreat	http://groveriverranch.com
Guard 1 Services	www.gaurd1services.com
Gull Lake Recreation Area	marykay.l.larson@usace.army.mil
Harlan County Lake	thomas.j.zikmund@usace.army.mil
Harry L. Englebright Lake	tom.bookholtz@usace.army.mil
Hartwell Lake	thomas.d.bowen@usace.army.mil
Havasu Riviera State Park	bworman@azstateparks.gov
Haw Creek Preserve State Park	https://volunteers.floridastateparks.org
Hearst San Simeon State Park	jared.meichtry@parks.ca.gov

Heber Dunes State Vehicle Recreation Area	james.claar@parks.ca.gov
Henderson Beach State Park	https://volunteers.floridastateparks.org
Hendy Woods State Park	alyson.fussell@parks.ca.gov
Hensley Lake/Hidden Dam	nicolas.r.figueroa@usace.army.mil
Heyburn Lake	john.r.hamblen@usace.army.mil
Highlands Hammock State Park	https://volunteers.floridastateparks.org
Hillsborough River State Park	https://volunteers.floridastateparks.org
Hillsdale Lake	james.d.bell@usace.army.mil
Holliday Lake State Park-	vspvolunteer@dcr.virginia.gov
Holt Lake/Black Warrior & Tombigbee Lakes	russell.b.barton@usace.army.mil
Homme Lake	christopher.m.botz@usace.army.mil
Homolovi State Park	bworman@azstateparks.gov
Honeymoon Island State Park	https://volunteers.floridastateparks.org
Hontoon Island State Park	https://volunteers.floridastateparks.org
Hoodoo Recreation Services	www.hoodoo.com
Hope Island	volunteers@parks.wa.gov
Hopkinton-Everett Lake	stephen.p.dermody@usace.army.mil
Hopper Bros Christmas Trees	www.hopperbros.com

Hords Creek Lake	brandon.l.moehrle@usace.army.mil
Horseshoe Trails Campground	www.horseshoetrailscamping.com
Hugh Taylor Birch State Park	https://volunteers.floridastateparks.org
Hugo Lake	sarah.m.whorton@usace.army.mil
Humboldt Redwoods State Park	vc@humboldtredwoods.org
Hungry Mother State Park	vspvolunteer@dcr.virginia.gov
Ichetucknee Springs State Park	https://volunteers.floridastateparks.org
Ichetucknee Trace	https://volunteers.floridastateparks.org
Ike Kinswa State Park	volunteers@parks.wa.gov
Illahee State Park	volunteers@parks.wa.gov
Illinois Waterway Farmdale/Fondulac	todd.d.ernenputsch@usace.army.mil
Illinois Waterway Visitor Center	gary.l.shea@usace.army.mil
Imperial Sand Dunes	www.isdpermits.net
Indian Grinding Rock State Historic Park	lee.eal@parks.ca.gov
Indian Key Historic State Park	https://volunteers.floridastateparks.org
Indian River Lagoon Preserve State Park	https://volunteers.floridastateparks.org
J. Edward Roush Lake	anthony.h.schoenecker@usace.army.mil
J. Percy Priest Lake	carter.robinson@usace.army.mil
Jack Island Preserve	https://volunteers.floridastateparks.org

Jacks Camper Sales	www.jackscampers.com
James River State Park	vspvolunteer@dcr.virginia.gov
Jarrell Cove State Park	volunteers@parks.wa.gov
Jedediah Smith Redwoods State Park	mike.whelan@parks.ca.gov
Jennings Randolph Lake	thomas.m.craig@usace.army.mil
Jesse Brent Lower Mississippi River Museum	aaron.w.posner@usace.army.mil
Jim Woodruff Lake & Dam	ruth.c.heying@usace.army.mil
Joe Pool Lake	jeremy.a.spencer@usace.army.mil
Joemma Beach State Park	volunteers@parks.wa.gov
John D. Macarthur Beach State Park	https://volunteers.floridastateparks.org
John Day Lock & Dam/Willow Creek Project	greg.m.volkman@usace.army.mil
John Gorrie Museum State Park	https://volunteers.floridastateparks.org
John H Kerr Dam And Reservoir	david.a.schwartz@usace.army.mil
John Martin Dam	jonathan.b.tague@usace.army.mil
John Paul Hammerschmidt Lake	donnie.l.lindsay@usace.army.mil
John Pennekamp Coral Reef State Park	https://volunteers.floridastateparks.org
John Redmond Lake	gary.a.kepley@usace.army.mil

John U. Lloyd Beach State Park	https://volunteers.floridastateparks.org
John W Flannagan Dam & Reservoir	marty.j.davis@usace.army.mil
Jonathan Dickinson State Park	https://volunteers.floridastateparks.org
Judah P. Benjamin Confederate Memorial At Gamble Plantation Historic State Park	https://volunteers.floridastateparks.org
Kampgrounds Enterprises, Inc	http://www.keioutdoor.com/
Kanaskat-Palmer State Park	volunteers@parks.wa.gov
Kanopolis Lake	brock.a.delong@usace.army.mil
Kartchner Caverns State Park	bworman@azstateparks.gov
Katherine Landing At Lake Mohave Marina	www.katherinelanding.com
Kaw Lake	dakota.l.allison@usace.army.mil
Kelly Dahl	www.americanll.com
Keystone Lake	john.r.hamblen@usace.army.mil or
Kinzua Dam/Allegheny Reservoir	steven.j.lauser@usace.army.mil
Kiptopeke State Park	vspvolunteer@dcr.virginia.gov
Kissimmee Prairie Preserve State Park	https://volunteers.floridastateparks.org
Kitchen Craft Cookware	https://kitchencraftcookware.com/
Kitsap Memorial State Park	volunteers@parks.wa.gov

Knightville Dam and Littleville Lake	matthew.s.coleman@usace.army.mil
Koreshan State Historic Site	https://volunteers.floridastateparks.org
Lac Qui Parle Lake	randy.d.melby@usace.army.mil
Lafayette Blue Springs State Park	https://volunteers.floridastateparks.org
Lake Anna State Park	vspvolunteer@dcr.virginia.gov
Lake Barkley	wesley.r.daveport@usace.army.mil
Lake Chabot	www.lakechabotrecreation.com
Lake Chelan State Park	volunteers@parks.wa.gov
Lake Cumberland	eric.t.matthews@usace.army.mil
Lake Easton State Park	volunteers@parks.wa.gov
Lake Georgetown	bradley.w.arldt@usace.army.mil
Lake Greeson	randy.m.sorrells@usace.army.mil
Lake Gregory Recreation Company	www.lakegregoryrecreation.com
Lake Griffin State Park	https://volunteers.floridastateparks.org
Lake Havasu State Park	bworman@azstateparks.gov
Lake Hemet	www.lakehemetrecreation.com
Lake Jackson Mounds Archaeological State Park	https://volunteers.floridastateparks.org
Lake June-In-Winter Scrub State Park	https://volunteers.floridastateparks.org

Lake Kaweah/Terminus Dam	robin.w.lebo@usace.army.mil
Lake Kissimmee State Park	https://volunteers.floridastateparks.org
Lake Louisa State Park	https://volunteers.floridastateparks.org
Lake Manatee State Park	https://volunteers.floridastateparks.org
Lake Mendocino/Coyote Valley Dam	poppy.l.lozoff@usace.army.mil
Lake Nacimiento	www.nacimientoresort.com
Lake O' The Pines/Ferrell's Bridge Dam	robert.l.henderson@usace.army.mil
Lake Oahe & Dam/Beaver Creek	john.f.voeller@usace.army.mil
Lake Oahe And Dam	phillip.r.sheffield@usace.army.mil
Lake Okeechobee Waterway	robert.r.hill@usace.army.mil
Lake Oroville State Recreation Area	christopher.beehner@parks.ca.gov
Lake Osprey Rv Resort	www.robertresorts.com
Lake Sacajawea / Ice Harbor Lock & Dam	heather.l.geertsen@usace.army.mil
Lake Sammamish State Park	volunteers@parks.wa.gov
Lake San Antonio	www.lakesanantonioresort.com
Lake Sharpe/Big Bend Project	robert.l.karlen@usace.army.mil
Lake Shelbyville	ashley.s.florey@usace.army.mil

Lake Sidney Lanier	daniel.l.brownlow@usace.army.mil
Lake Sonoma	emily.t.kohl@usace.army.mil
Lake State Park	volunteers@parks.wa.gov
Lake Sylvia State Park	volunteers@parks.wa.gov
Lake Talquin State Park	https://volunteers.floridastateparks.org
Lake Texoma	tanner.l.mcadams@usace.army.mil
Lake Washington Ship Canal/Hiram M. Chittenden Locks	kathryn.f.mcgillvray@usace.army.mil
Lake Wenatchee State Park	volunteers@parks.wa.gov
Lakes/Dry Falls Visitor Center	volunteers@parks.wa.gov
Larrabee State Park	volunteers@parks.wa.gov
Lassen Café & Gift, Lassen Volcanic National Park	www.lassenrecreation.com
Laurel River Lake	robert.r.hill@usace.army.mil
Lavon Lake	jonathan.e.boyce@usace.army.mil
Leaf Verde RR Resort	http://www.leafverde.com
Leech Lake	gus.garbe@usace.army.mil
Leesville Lake	lydia.e.fach@usace.army.mil
Leisure Resort	http://www.leisurecamp.net
Leo Carillo State Park	lee.hawkins@parks.ca.gov
Letchworth-Love Mounds Archaeological State Park	https://volunteers.floridastateparks.org

Lewis And Clark State Park	volunteers@parks.wa.gov
Lewis And Clark Trail State Park	volunteers@parks.wa.gov
Lewisville Lake/Ray Roberts Lake	james.m.stegall@usace.army.mil
Libby Dam/Lake Koocanusa	susan.j.james@usace.army.mil
Lignumvitae Key Botanical State Park	https://volunteers.floridastateparks.org
Lime Kiln State Park	volunteers@parks.wa.gov
Lincoln Rock State Park	volunteers@parks.wa.gov
Little Basin Group Campground	www.littlebasin.org
Little Lake	www.lakehemetrecreation.com/littlelake
Little Manatee River State Park	https://volunteers.floridastateparks.org
Little Rock District Office	chris.l.smith@usace.army.mil
Little Talbot Island State Park	https://volunteers.floridastateparks.org
Long Branch Lake	michael.p.kuntz@usace.army.mil
Long Key State Park	https://volunteers.floridastateparks.org
Long Lake Trailhead	www.americanll.com
Lookout Point Lake	donna.r.bryant@usace.army.mil
Loon Lake Campground	www.americanll.com
Los Vaqueros Watershed	www.norcalfishing.com/los_vaqueros
Lost Creek Lake	anthony.j.johnson@usace.army.mil

Lost Dutchman State Park	bworman@azstateparks.gov
Louisville District Office	clifton.r.kilpatrick@usace.army.mil
Lovers Key State Park	https://volunteers.floridastateparks.org
Lower Granite Lock & Dam Natural Resource Office/Lower Granite Lake	dawn.waldal@usace.army.mil
Lower Wekiva River Preserve State Park	https://volunteers.floridastateparks.org
Loyalhanna Lake	ben.a.caparelli@usace.army.mil
Lt. Blender Cocktails	http://ltblender.com
Lucky Peak Lake & Dam	keith.b.hyde@usace.army.mil
Lyman Lake State Park	bworman@azstateparks.gov
Lyons Ferry	volunteers@parks.wa.gov
Mackerricher State Park	alyson.fussell@parks.ca.gov
Madira Bickel Mound State Archaeological Site	https://volunteers.floridastateparks.org
Madison Blue Spring State Park	https://volunteers.floridastateparks.org
Mahoning Creek Lake	grover.m.pegg@usace.army.mil
Malakof Diggins State Historic Park-	brooke.betz@parks.ca.gov
Malibu Creek State Park	lee.hawkins@parks.ca.gov

Manatee Springs State Park	https://volunteers.floridastateparks.org
Manchester State Park	alyson.fussell@parks.ca.gov
Manchester State Park	volunteers@parks.wa.gov
Manresa State Beach	arlene.shaffer@parks.ca.gov
Mansfield Hollow Lake	michelle.l.cucchi@usace.army.mil
Manzanita Lake Camper Service Store	www.lassenrecreation.com
Maple Grove Koa	https://koa.com/campgrounds/minneapolis-northwest/
Marion Reservoir	scott.a.mccrone@usace.army.mil
Marjorie Harris Carr Cross Florida Greenway	https://volunteers.floridastateparks.org
Marjorie Kinnan Rawlings Historic State Park	https://volunteers.floridastateparks.org
Martins Fork Lake	david.c.robinson@usace.army.mil
Martis Creek Lake	jason.c.worden@usace.army.mil
Maryhill State Park	volunteers@parks.wa.gov
Mcfarland State Historic Park	bworman@azstateparks.gov
Mcgrath State Beach	jeffrey.langley@parks.ca.gov
Mcnary Lock & Dam/Lake Wallula	david.f.mcdermott@usace.army.mil
Meeker Park Campground	www.americanll.com
Melvern Lake	buck.a.walker@usace.army.mil

Mendocino Headlands State Park	fordhouse@mcn.org
Michael J. Kirwan Dam	julie.r.stone@usace.army.mil
Mike Roess Gold Head Branch State Park	https://volunteers.floridastateparks.org
Milford Lake	blake.d.mcpherren@usace.army.mil
Mill Creek Dam/Bennington Lake	cady.l.tyron@usace.army.mil
Millersylvania State Park	volunteers@parks.wa.gov
Millerton Lake State Recreation Area	www.parks.ca.gov/millertonlake
Millwood Lake	brooke.s.kervin@usace.army.mil
Mississinewa Lake	gregory.n.carpenter@usace.army.mil
Mississippi River Project Pool	bret.r.streckwald@usace.army.mil
Mississippi River Project Pool:Shady Creek Recreation Area	jacob.j.kresel@usace.army.mil
Mitchell Lake Trailhead	www.americanll.com
Mobile District Office	consuela.a.gunter@usace.army.mil
Mohawk Dam/North Branch Kokosing	bryan.r.muroski@usace.army.mil
Mohicanville Dam	bryan.r.muroski@usace.army.mil
Monroe Lake	gary.j.staigl@usace.army.mil
Monroe Navigation Project	diane.golden@usace.army.mil

Montana De Oro State Park	jennifer.wilson@parks.ca.gov
Monterey County Parks	www.co.monterey.ca.us/parks
Moran State Park	volunteers@parks.wa.gov
Morro Bay State Park	jennifer.wilson@parks.ca.gov
Mosquito Creek Lake	kathryn.fatula@usace.army.mil
Mound Key Archaeological State Park	https://volunteers.floridastateparks.org
Mount Morris Dam	juliana.e.smith@usace.army.mil
Mount Rushmore Resort And Lodge At Palmer Gulch	http://www.palmergulch.com/
Mt St Helens Visitors Center	volunteers@parks.wa.gov
Mt St Helens Visitors Center	volunteers@parks.wa.gov
Mud Mountain Dam	laura.g.robinson@usace.army.mil
Myakka River State Park	https://volunteers.floridastateparks.org
Myrtle Beach State Park – Nature Center	https://southcarolinaparks.com/myrtle-beach
Mystery Bay State Park	fwv390@parks.wa.gov
Mystery Bay-Fort Flagler	volunteers@parks.wa.gov
National Great Rivers Museum	janet.k.meredith@usace.army.mil
Natural Bridge Battlefield Historic State Park	https://volunteers.floridastateparks.org

Natural Bridge State Park	vspvolunteer@dcr.virginia.gov
Natural Tunnel State Park	vspvolunteer@dcr.virginia.gov
Nature Coast State Trail	https://volunteers.floridastateparks.org
Naugatuck River Basin	marissa.l.wright@usace.army.mil
Navarro Mills Lake	teresa.j.ezersky@usace.army.mil
New Hogan Lake	allen.a.aguas@usace.army.mil
Newt Graham Lock & Dam	joshua.w.mathis@usace.army.mil
Next Day Funding	www.nextdayfunders.com
Nimrod Lake	lisa.a.owens@usace.army.mil
Nolin River Lake	jon.p.fillingham@usace.army.mil
Nolte State Park	volunteers@parks.wa.gov
Nolte State Park	volunteers@parks.wa.gov
Norfork Lakes & Bull Shoals	kevin.patterson@usace.army.mil
North Fork Of The Pound River	marty.j.davis@usace.army.mil
North Hartland Lake	heather.l.morse@usace.army.mil
North Lake Rv Park And Campground	http://www.northlakervparkandcampground.com
North Peninsula State Park	https://volunteers.floridastateparks.org
O'leno State Park	https://volunteers.floridastateparks.org
Ocala North Rv Park	http://www.ocalanorthrv.com/
Occoneechee State Park	vspvolunteer@dcr.virginia.gov
Ocean City State Park	volunteers@parks.wa.gov

Ocean Waves Campground	www.oceanwavescampground.com
Ochlockonee River State Park	https://volunteers.floridastateparks.org
Okatibbee Lake	nikia.r.angevine@usace.army.mil
Okeechobee Battlefield Historic State Park	https://volunteers.floridastateparks.org
Olallie State Park	volunteers@parks.wa.gov
Old Hickory Lake	dylon.j.anderson@usace.army.mil
Old River Control Project	clyde.j.harvey@usace.army.mil
Oleta River State Park	https://volunteers.floridastateparks.org
Olive Ridge	www.americanll.com
Olustee Battlefield Historic State Park	https://volunteers.floridastateparks.org
Omaha District Office	harold.m.key@usace.army.mil
Oologah Lake	jason.a.person@usace.army.mil
Orman House Historic State Park	https://volunteers.floridastateparks.org
Orwell Lake	randy.d.melby@usace.army.mil
Oscar Scherer State Park	https://volunteers.floridastateparks.org
Otter Brook/Surry Mountain Lakes	christie.l.baker@usace.army.mil
Ouachita Lake	amy.j.shultz@usace.army.mil
Ozark Lake	donnie.ll.lindsay@usace.army.mil
Pacific Beach State Park	volunteers@parks.wa.gov
Paint Creek Lake	connor.s.santee@usace.army.mil
Paintsville Lake	nathan.a.shelton@usace.army.mil

Palatka-To-Lake Butler State Trail	https://volunteers.floridastateparks.org
Palatka-To-St. Augustine State Trail	https://volunteers.floridastateparks.org
Palm Springs/Joshua Tree Koa	www.keioutdoorjobs.com
Palm View Gardens Rv Resort	https://www.rvresorts.com/palm-view-gardens.html
Palomar Mountain State Park	jessica.murany@parks.ca.gov
Paradise Point State Park	volunteers@parks.wa.gov
Pat Mayse Lake	sarah.k.noel@usace.army.mil
Patagonia Lake State Park	bworman@azstateparks.gov
Patoka Lake	john.l.hovis@usace.army.mil
Patrick's Point State Park	maury.morningstar@parks.ca.gov
Pawnee Campground	www.americanll.com
Paynes Creek Historic State Park	https://volunteers.floridastateparks.org
Paynes Prairie Preserve State Park	https://volunteers.floridastateparks.org
Peace Arch State Park	volunteers@parks.wa.gov
Peaceful Valley Campground	www.americanll.com
Pearson-Skubitz Big Hill Lake	barbara.j.busenbarrick@usace.army.mil
Penrose Point State Park	volunteers@parks.wa.gov
Perdido Key State Park	https://volunteers.floridastateparks.org

Perry Lake	wesley.j.henson@usace.army.mil
Pfeiffer Big Sur State Park	sharon.pieniak@parks.ca.gov
Philadelphia District Office	nathan.t.freiwald@usace.army.mil
Philpott Lake	richard.a.wigley@usace.army.mil
Picacho Peak State Park	bworman@azstateparks.gov
Pine Creek Lake	corey.claborn@usace.army.mil
Pine Flat Lake & Dam	isac.g.hermosilla@usace.army.mil
Pipestem Lake	robert.j.martin@usace.army.mil
Pismo State Beach	jorge.barajas-ochoa@parks.ca.gov
Pleasant Hill Lake	bryan.r.muroski@usace.army.mil
Plumas-Eureka State Park	scott.elliott@parks.ca.gov
Pocahontas State Park	vspvolunteer@dcr.virginia.gov
Point Mugu State Park	lee.hawkins@parks.ca.gov
Pokegama Lake & Dam/Winnie Dam	jeff.j.cook@usace.army.mil
Pomme De Terre Lake	devin.t.holt@usace.army.mil
Pomona Lake	william.k.bolt@usace.army.mil
Ponce De Leon Springs State Park	https://volunteers.floridastateparks.org
Ponderosa Cove	www.americanll.com
Portola Redwoods State Park	tyler.knapp@parks.ca.gov
Potholes State Park	volunteers@parks.wa.gov
Potlatch State Park	volunteers@parks.wa.gov

Powhatan State Park -	vspvolunteer@dcr.virginia.gov
Prairie Creek Redwoods State Park	leslie.reyes@parks.ca.gov
Price's Scrub	https://volunteers.floridastateparks.org
Proctor Lake	stephanie.a.jones@usace.army.mil
Pumpkin Hill Creek Preserve State Park	https://volunteers.floridastateparks.org
Quagga Inspection Services, Llc	www.quaggainspections.com
R.D. Bailey Lake	johnathan.a.browning@usace.army.mil
Rainbow Falls State Park Rasar State Park	volunteers@parks.wa.gov
Rainbow Lakes Campground	www.americanll.com
Rainbow Springs State Park	https://volunteers.floridastateparks.org
Rainier Guest Services	http://mtrainierguestservices.com/about-us/careers/
Rathbun Lake	john.p.pasa@usace.army.mil
Ravine Gardens State Park	https://volunteers.floridastateparks.org
Raystown Lake	alicia.e.wicker@usace.army.mil
Red Rock Lake	mark.r.pollastrini@usace.army.mil
Red Rock State Park	bworman@azstateparks.gov
Refugio State Beach	scott.anderson@parks.ca.gov
Rend Lake	cassie.l.magsig@usace.army.mil
Richard B. Russell Dam & Lake	zachary.e.baldwin@usace.army.mil
Richardson Grove State Park	vc@humboldtredwoods.org

Riordan Mansion State Historic Park	bworman@azstateparks.gov
River Island State Park	bworman@azstateparks.gov
River Rise Preserve State Park	https://volunteers.floridastateparks.org
Rivers Project Office	angela.smith@usace.army.mil
Riverside State Park	volunteers@parks.wa.gov
Rock Shadows Rv Resort	http://www.rockshadows.com
Rock Springs Run State Reserve	https://volunteers.floridastateparks.org
Rockin' River Ranch State Park	bworman@azstateparks.gov
Rockport State Park	volunteers@parks.wa.gov
Rogue River Basin Project	joyce.a.szalwinsii@usace.army.mil
Roman Nose State Park	kyle.bernis@travelok.com
Roper Lake State Park	bworman@azstateparks.gov
Rough River Lake	adam.d.taylor@usace.army.mil
Russellville Project: Dardanelle Lake	scott.j.fryer@usace.army.mil
Russian Gulch State Park	alyson.fussell@parks.ca.gov
Rv Transport Inc	www.rvtransport.com
Rving Lifestyle Ambassadors	www.rvingnetwork.com
Sacajawea State Park	volunteers@parks.wa.gov
Sacramento District Office	alicia.s.unsinn@usace.army.mil

Saddleback Butte State Park	kevin.overduin@parks.ca.gov
Saint Paul District Office	tamryn.johnson@usace.army.mil
Salamonie Lake	john.d.scheiber@usace.army.mil
Salt Point State Park	trevor.nealy@parks.ca.gov
Salton Sea SRA	salton.sea@parks.ca.gov
Saltwater State Park	volunteers@parks.wa.gov
Sam Rayburn Reservoir	cody.l.turner@usace.army.mil
San Diego County Parks	www.sdparks.org
San Felasco Hammock Preserve State Park	https://volunteers.floridastateparks.org
San Francisco Bay Model Visitor Center	joanne.jarvis@usace.army.mil
San Francisco District Office-Nrs Office/Warm Springs Dam	charles.fenwick@usace.army.mil
San Marcos De Apalache Historic State Park	https://volunteers.floridastateparks.org
San Pedro Underwater Archaeological Preserve State Park	https://volunteers.floridastateparks.org
San Rafael State Natural Area	bworman@azstateparks.gov
San Simeon Campground	jared.meichtry@parks.ca.gov
Sand Flat Campground	www.americanll.com

Sandy Lake & Dam	courtney.m.kinnett@usace.army.mil
Santa Rosa Lake	paul.d.sanchez@usace.army.mil
Sardis Lake	chris.r.gurner@usace.army.mil
Sardis Lake	shae.harrison@usace.army.mil
Savannah District Office	ryan.d.hartwig@usace.army.mil
Savannah District Office	joseph.w.melton@usace.army.mil
Savannas Preserve State Park	https://volunteers.floridastateparks.org
Saylorville Lake	emma.m.nelson@usace.army.mil
Scenic Beach State Park	volunteers@parks.wa.gov
Scenic Canyons Recreational Services	www.sceniccanyons.com
Schafer State Park	volunteers@parks.wa.gov
Seabranch Preserve State Park	https://volunteers.floridastateparks.org
Seaquest State Park	volunteers@parks.wa.gov
Seattle District Office	taylor.m.johnson@usace.army.mil
Sebastian Inlet State Park	https://volunteers.floridastateparks.org
Sequim Bay (Ramblewood)	volunteers@parks.wa.gov
Sequim Bay State Park	volunteers@parks.wa.gov
Shasta Recreation Company	www.shastatrinitycamping.com
Shenandoah River State Park	vspvolunteer@dcr.virginia.gov
Shenango River Lake	jason.cote@usace.army.mil

Signal Mountain Lodge	http://www.workatsignal.com/
Silver Falls Lodge & Conference Center	www.silverfallslodge.com
Silver Fork Campground	www.americanll.com
Silver Springs State Park	https://volunteers.floridastateparks.org
Skiatook Lake	jeff.walker@usace.army.mil
Sky Valley Resorts	www.skyvalleyresorts.com
Skyline Ranch Rv Park	http://www.skylineranchrvpark.com
Skyway Fishing Pier State Park	https://volunteers.floridastateparks.org
Smith Mountain Lake State Park	vspvolunteer@dcr.virginia.gov
Smithville Lake	jaime.d.picken@usace.army.mil
Somerville Lake	jennifer.r.schultz.plair@usace.army.mil
Sonoita Creek State Natural Area	bworman@azstateparks.gov
Southeast Publications	www.southeastpublications.com
Southern Cross	www.southerncrossinc.com
Southfork State Park	https://volunteers.floridastateparks.org
Spencer Spit State Park	volunteers@parks.wa.gov
Spruce Lake Rv Resort	https://sprucelakerv.com/
Square Lake State Park	volunteers@parks.wa.gov
Squilchuck State Park	volunteers@parks.wa.gov
St. Andrews State Park	https://volunteers.floridastateparks.org

St. Louis District Office	jonathan.w.schulte@usace.army.mil
St. Lucie Inlet Preserve State Park	https://volunteers.floridastateparks.org
St. Marks River State Park	https://volunteers.floridastateparks.org
St. Sebastian River Preserve State Park	https://volunteers.floridastateparks.org
Stanislaus National Forest	www.americanll.com
Stanislaus River Parks	hilary.a.coleman@usace.army.mil
State Park Olmstead State Park	volunteers@parks.wa.gov
Staunton River State Park	vspvolunteer@dcr.virginia.gov
Steamboat Rock State Park	volunteers@parks.wa.gov
Stephen Foster Folk Culture Center State Park	https://volunteers.floridastateparks.org
Stockton Lake	derrick.s.phillips@usace.army.mil
Stonewall Jackson Lake	christopher.s.hannah@usace.army.mil
Stony Brook Recreation And Camping	www.stonybrookrec.com
Strates Shows, Inc. Carnivals	www.strates.com
Stump Pass Beach State Park	https://volunteers.floridastateparks.org
Stumpy Meadows Campground	www.americanll.com
Success Lake	robert.moreno@usace.army.mil

Sucia Island State Park	volunteers@parks.wa.gov
Sucia Island State Park	volunteers@parks.wa.gov
Sugar Barge Resort & Marina	www.sugarbarge.com
Sugar Pine Point State Park	steven.oriol@parks.ca.gov
Summersville Lake	michael.l.mccoy@usace.army.mil
Sun Lakes/Dry Falls State Park	volunteers@parks.wa.gov
Sunset Campground	www.americanll.com
Sutton Lake	keith.a.nuckles@usace.army.mil
Suwannee River State Park	https://volunteers.floridastateparks.org
Suwannee River Wilderness Trail	https://volunteers.floridastateparks.org
Sweetwater Campground	www.americanll.com
T. H. Stone Memorial St. Joseph Peninsula State Park	https://volunteers.floridastateparks.org
Table Rock Lake	emily.t.wooldridge@usace.army.mil
Talbot Islands Geopark	https://volunteers.floridastateparks.org
Talkeetna Alaskan Lodge	http://www.alaskacollection.com/corporate/careers/
Tallahassee-St. Marks Geo Park	https://volunteers.floridastateparks.org
Tallahassee-St. Marks Historic Railroad State Trail	https://volunteers.floridastateparks.org
Tarkiln Bayou Preserve State Park	https://volunteers.floridastateparks.org

Taylorsville Lake	evan.s.mckinney@usace.army.mil
Tenkiller Ferry Lake/Webbers Falls Pool	brent.c.buford@usace.army.mil
Tennessee Tombigbee Waterway-Bay Springs	steven.c.koon@usace.army.mil
Tennessee Tombigbee-Aberdeen/Columbus	adam.r.prentice@usace.army.mil
Tennessee-Tombigbee Waterway/Tom Bevill Visitor Center	adam.r.prentice@usace.army.mil
Terra Ceia Preserve State Park	https://volunteers.floridastateparks.org
Texas Trails Rv Resort	www.texastrailsrv.com
The Barnacle Historic State Park	https://volunteers.floridastateparks.org
The California Parkscompany	www.calparksco.com
The Dalles Lock & Dam/Lake Celilo	amber.c.tilton@usace.army.mil
The Lemon Cove Village RV Park	http://lemoncovevillagervpark.com
The Lodges Of The Northern Big Horn Mountains	http://lodgesofthenorthernbighornmountains.com/
The Ranch At Little Hills	www.littlehillsweddings.com
Theodore Roosevelt Medora Foundation	http://www.medora.com/employment/
Three Rivers State Park	https://volunteers.floridastateparks.org

Time Keepers Security Mgt.	info@tieronegroup.com
Tioga-Hammond & Cowanesque Lake	molly.a.wilson@usace.army.mil
Tionesta Lake	jason.a.bowers@usace.army.mil
Toad Suck Ferry L/D/Maumelle Park	thomas.ryan.king@usace.army.mil
Tom Jenkins Dam	robert.w.cifranic@usace.army.mil
Tomoka State Park	https://volunteers.floridastateparks.org
Top Of The Hill RV Resort	www.topofthehillrvresort.com
Topsail Hill Preserve State Park	https://volunteers.floridastateparks.org
Torreya State Park	https://volunteers.floridastateparks.org
Town Bluff Dam/B.A.Steinhagen Lake	cody.l.turner@usace.army.mil
Tri-Lakes	timothy.a.rose@usace.army.mil
Troy Spring State Park	https://volunteers.floridastateparks.org
Tully Lake	jeffrey.c.mangum@usace.army.mil
Tulsa District Office	jason.m.knight@usace.army.mil
Turlock SRA	www.americanll.com
Tuttle Creek Lake	angelia.j.lentz@usace.army.mil
Twanoh State Park	volunteers@parks.wa.gov
Twenty-Five Mile Creek State Park	volunteers@parks.wa.gov
Twin Harbors State Park	volunteers@parks.wa.gov
Tygart Lake	stacy.e.lewis@usace.army.mil
UPC Gate Services	www.upcgate.com
Upper Mississippi River Pool #1-10	randall.r.urich@usace.army.mil

USACE Volunteers	www.corpslakes.us/volunteer
USI RV Park	usirvpark.com
Vail Lake Resort	www.vaillakeresort.com
Valley View Christmas Trees	www.valleyviewchristmastrees.org
Van Horn Texas RV Park	http://www.vanhorntexasrvpark.com
Vandamme State Park	alyson.fussell@parks.ca.gov
Ventures West Inc.	http://www.ventureswestinc.com/
Verde River Greenway State Natural Area	bworman@azstateparks.gov
Verde Valley Archaeology Center	https://www.verdevalleyarchaeology.org
Vern Whitaker Horse Camp	norbert.ruhmke@parks.ca.gov
Vicksburg District Office	jonathan.d.harrell@usace.army.mil
W. Kerr Scott Dam & Reservoir	johnny.e.jones@usace.army.mil
Waccasassa Bay Preserve State Park	https://volunteers.floridastateparks.org
Waco Lake	michael.j.champagne@usace.army.mil
Wales West Rv Resort	www.waleswest.com
Wall Drug	http://www.walldrug.com/about-us/employment
Walla Walla District Office	michael.j.swenson@usace.army.mil
Wallace Falls State Park	volunteers@parks.wa.gov
Walter F. George Lake	william.a.hancock@usace.army.mil

Wanapum State Park	volunteers@parks.wa.gov
Wappapello Lake Management	rachel.r.lemons@usace.army.mil
Washington Oaks Gardens State Park	https://volunteers.floridastateparks.org
Wassamki Springs Campground	www.wassamkisprings.com
Waurika Lake Office	luke.t.prichard@usace.army.mil
Weeki Wachee Springs State Park	https://volunteers.floridastateparks.org
Wekiwa Springs State Park	https://volunteers.floridastateparks.org
Wellington Camping Park	www.wellingtoncampingparkleenh.com
Wenatchee Confluence State Park	volunteers@parks.wa.gov
Wench Creek Campground	www.americanll.com
Werner-Boyce Salt Springs State Park	https://volunteers.floridastateparks.org
Wes Skiles Peacock Springs State Park	https://volunteers.floridastateparks.org
West Fork Lake	stephanie.a.ison@usace.army.mil
West Hill Dam/Charles River	viola.m.bramel@usace.army.mil
West Point Lake	steven.m.rector@usace.army.mil
West Thompson Lake	michelle.l.cucchi@usace.army.mil
Westmoreland State Park	vspvolunteer@dcr.virginia.gov
Westport Union-Landing State Beach	alyson.fussell@parks.ca.gov

Westville Lake	keith.w.beecher@usace.army.mil
Whitney Lake Project Office/Aquilla Dam & Lake	jarod.d.briscoe@usace.army.mil
Wild Horse Project	http://wildhorseproject.org
William H Harsha Lake	samantha.k.bachelder@usace.army.mil
Wilson Lake	zach.d.hlad@usace.army.mil
Windley Key Fossil Reef Geological State Park	https://volunteers.floridastateparks.org
Wingate Creek State Park	https://volunteers.floridastateparks.org
Withlacoochee State Trail	https://volunteers.floridastateparks.org
Wolf Creek Campground	www.americanll.com
Wolf Creek National Fish Hatchery	https://www.fws.gov/wolfcreek
Woodcock Creek Lake & Union City Dam	joseph.d.arnett@usace.army.mil
Woodruff Lake	myers.hawkins@usace.army.mil
Woodson Bridge SRA	www.americanll.com
Wright Patman Lake	james.m.bransford@usace.army.mil
Xanterra Travel Collection	https://www.xanterra.com/who-we-are/careers/
Yakima Sportsman State Park	volunteers@parks.wa.gov
Yatesville Lake	andrew.j.auxier@usace.army.mil
Ybor City Museum State Park	https://volunteers.floridastateparks.org

Yellow Bluff Fort Historic State Park	https://volunteers.floridastateparks.org
Yellow River Marsh Preserve State Park	https://volunteers.floridastateparks.org
Yellowjacket Campground	www.americanll.com
Yellowstone Forever	www.yellowstone.org
Yellowstone General Stores	ygsjobs@delawarenorth.com
Yellowstone Golf Resort	http://www.yellowstonegolfresort.com
Yellowstone National Park Lodges	http://www.yellowstonejobs.com/
Yellowstone Park Service Stations Inc.	http://ypss.com/
Yellowstone Vacations	https://www.yellowstonevacations.com/jobs/west-yellowstone-jobs
YMCA Of The Rockies	http://workintherockies.org/
Youghiogheny River Lake	vincent.klinkner@usace.army.mil
Yulee Sugar Mill Ruins Historic State Park	https://volunteers.floridastateparks.org
Yuma Quartermaster Depot State Historic Park	bworman@azstateparks.gov
Yuma Territorial Prison State Historic Park	bworman@azstateparks.gov
Zion Mountain Ranch	careers@zmr.com

Part 5: Additional Resources

Common Interview Questions

Questions to Ask Employers

Websites for Job Listings

Sample Work Agreement

RV Glossary

Common Interview Questions

- How did you hear about this position?
- Describe yourself in 3 words.
- Why should we hire you?
- Why are you interested in working for us?
- What are your strengths/weaknesses?
- Name three things you would like to improve on?
- Are you willing to work holidays/weekends?
- Are you able to commit to the entire season?
- What are your salary requirements?
- Are you willing to work 40+ hours a week?
- Are you a leader or a follower?
- Tell me about an accomplishment you are most proud of.
- Tell me about a time you made a mistake and how you fixed it.
- Tell me about a time you handled a difficult situation and the outcome.
- Tell me about a time you had to deal with an angry or irate customer?
- How do you handle pressure?
- Explain the gap in your employment between these two dates?
- What questions do you have for me?

Questions for Employers

- What exactly does this position entail?
- What are the start and end dates of this position?
- How far in advance can we occupy the site?
- Do you offer a completion bonus?
- Is there a set schedule or rotating schedule?
- What type of training is provided?
- What is the dress code? Are uniforms provided?
- Are all hours paid? How many for the site?
- Are extra hours provided at pay? How many?
- Is overtime available? Mandatory? How much?
- Will couples work the same hours/days and off days?
- Can couples request opposite shifts and off days?
- Weekend/Nights/early mornings/holidays?
- What additional benefits are provided?
- How many other Workampers do you have?
- How many are returning Workampers?
- Do Workamper sites have full hookups?
- Are Workamper sites separate from daily guests?
- How is cell service in your area? Best carriers?
- How far is shopping? Groceries? Hospital? Gas? Walmart?
- Do you allow onsite RV washing and/or repairs?
- What is the percentage of guests for daily, seasonal, monthly and annual campers?
- Do you have any Workamper references I can follow-up with?

Sites for Job Listings

You can find job posting all over the web and while it's easy to just pull up a free job site and start applying, I want to caution you against believing everything you see advertised. Ads are not always verified for legitimacy, so just keep some level of skepticism. If an offer seems too good to be true… it probably is.

- https://www.workamper.com
- http://www.workampingjobs.com
- https://www.coolworks.com
- https://www.work-for-rvers-and-campers.com
- https://www.happyvagabonds.com
- https://workingcouples.com
- https://cfaia.catsone.com/careers/
- http://www.camphost.org
- http://www.camphost.org
- https://www.rvproperty.com/campground-jobs/
- https://www.rvparkstore.com/rv-park-help-wanted
- http://www.americanll.com

You can also check out larger job board sites and search for keywords like 'campground' and 'park host'

- https://www.usajobs.gov
- https://www.indeed.com
- https://www.volunteer.gov

Sample Work Agreement

September 9, 2018

Mrs. Employer
Company Name
1234 First Street
Anytown, State ZIP

Dear Mr & Mrs Workamper

We are excited you have agreed to join our team for the upcoming season! As a measure of good faith we ask that you read the following work agreement and provide a signed copy for our files.

Your position will start on March 3, 2019 and end   September 9, 2019. You are welcome to arrive up to five days in advance and stay an additional 5 days after your position ends.

Your site will be provided for FREE and will not be included in your wages on your W-2 statement, since we require you to stay onsite. The space we have reserved is site #512 and includes water, sewer, electric, cable and Wi-Fi.

You have agreed to work in our front office, as a Reservation Agent booking reservations for our guests and answering customer phone calls. Your schedule will rotate weekly, but you will work between 30-40 hours each week at a rate of 11.50 per hour.

We also pay a completion bonus at the end of the season, which is calculated at $1 for every hour worked.

Please sign and return a copy of this letter by fax or mail no later than September 15, 2018 .

We agree to the terms outline above:

_____   _____
Mrs. Employer Signature   Date   Mrs. Workamper Signature   Date

257

RV Glossary

ARVC: National Association of RV Parks & Campgrounds

BLM: Bureau of Land Management

Black Water: Sewage

Blueboy: A portable waste tank, usually blue in color.

Boondocking: Camping without utilizes.

Bunkhouse: RV models with bunkbeds.

Class A: Motorhome usually ranging from 26-40 feet in length.

Class B: Smaller van-like motorhomes.

Class C: Motorhome with cab section over driving area for sleeping or sometimes entertainment and storage.

Corps/USACE: US Army Corps of Engineers

Dry Camping: Boondocking- Camping without utilizes.

DOE: Depending On Experience

DW: Dry weight- the weight of the RV without supplies or passengers.

EOE: Equal Opportunity Employer

Extended Stay: Sites reserved for RVers who wish to stay for longer periods of time. Usually monthly or season.

FHU: Full hookups (water, electric, sewer)

Fifth-Wheel: Pull behind RV type with special hitch inside the bed of a pickup truck.

FMCA: Family Motor Coach Association

Fresh Water: Water that is safe to drink.

Full-time: Traveling in an RV year-round.

Full-timer: Someone who lives in their RV full time

Galley: RV Kitchen

Grey Water: Used water from the kitchen, bathroom sinks and shower.

Hitch: Joint that is used to secure two vehicles for towing capability.

Hookups: Utilities like electric, water, sewer, and cable.

KOA: Kampgrounds of America- franchise of RV Parks

Locals: Refers to the local community. Non-RVers

NPS: National Park Service

Rig: Another term to describe your RV setup.

RV: Travel trailer, motorhome or 5th-wheel

RVIA: Recreation Vehicle Industry Association

Shore Power: Electricity provided by an external source.

Snowbirds: RVers who go South each winter

Sticks and Bricks: Traditional housing options.

Stipend: Fixed amount of money for expenses (i.e. food, fuel, etc.) paid to volunteers at government agencies or non-profits

Toad: Tow vehicle

Toy Hauler: RV with built in cargo space

Travel Trailer: Non-motorized RV units that need to be towed by a truck or large SUV.

TT: Thousand Trails Membership Club

USFS: U.S. Forest Service

USFWS: U.S. Fish & Wildlife Service

Volunteer: An individual who performs hours of service for a public agency or non-profit organization for civic, charitable, or humanitarian reasons

W/E/S: Water/Electric/Sewer

Wi-Fi: Wireless Internet Access

Winterize: Special steps to prepare the RV for Winter use and/or storage.

Workamper: Adventuresome individuals, couples and families who have chosen a wonderful lifestyle that combines ANY kind of part-time or full-time work with RV camping. If you work as an employee, operate a business, or donate your time as a volunteer, AND you sleep in an RV, you are a Workamper!

_ _ 与 A _ エ

Epilogue

When I look back on our decision to travel full-time and live in an RV, sometimes it still surprises me that we actually did it! I mean there are many things we've wanted to do in life, including living on a sailboat, that we just haven't had the nerve to actually follow through with. Fortunately, RV life was not one of them!

Living life on the road was a radical change for us and even more so for our family and friends, none of which live lives similar to ours. We didn't let negative comments or fear of the unknown stand in our way, and I firmly believe you should not either!

Over the past 5 years, we've had the privilege to visit over 30 states with our children and actually explore like locals, rather than tourists. We've met great people, seen some amazing new places, and done some pretty incredible things together as a family. These memories will stay with us for years to come and in all honesty, I have to admit this is by far the best part of going full-time.

We've met many people along our journey who praise the decision to go RVing at a younger age than traditionally acceptable. We were in our 20's when we started and although we didn't have the biggest or prettiest RV available (we actually had the opposite) we didn't care! We wanted to travel and try something new, so we made it happen! I'm always honest about this, and I'll say it again-it wasn't a walk in the park to learn how to RV, then adjust to living in one, and then figure out how to make money to keep the adventures going, but I wouldn't choose any other way!

So whatever age you are, if you are considering RV lifestyle and have a dream of traveling, I'd like to leave you with one piece of advice...

Go Small & Go Now!

Take a chance on adventure! Find a way that's comfortable and find a way to maintain it. Then set a date and just do it. Conquer your fears, prove your naysayers wrong and achieve this goal you set for yourself by any means necessary!

As always,

Safe Travels & Many Adventures

-Sharee

About the Author

5 years ago, my husband Antwon & I decided to try something crazy and way outside of our comfort zone. We decided to buy an RV and live it in with our 4 kids.

Since that moment, life has taken us on some pretty epic adventures and I went from not knowing what Workamping was to writing articles about it while we experienced the lifestyle first hand, to now working behind the scenes as the Director of Operations for Workamper News, where I help connect both sides of the Workamping community and encourage growth and new opportunities from within.

I'm also a travel blogger and entrepreneur. I love to create products and services to help others be successful in the RV lifestyle and am currently working on building my own RV community website focusing on delivering incredible content and resources to folks who love to explore, with a focus on where to go and what to do!

Stay in touch on Facebook @LiveCampWork &

Check out www.LiveCampWork.com

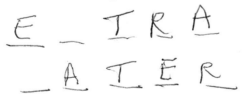

SPIRIT ↓ ~~802 210 333~~

＊ A9P68Y

211·17

SPIRIT # 800 772-7117

Booking.COM CONF No.
cancellation

211
52
———
263

3113004278 PIN 8635

48763

HDTKYM   1.19 SPIRIT

＊ 11ZRNN   52.00 SPIRIT

_ E D A _   _ E _ A D

FRONTIER   P6M17F
              ~~P6M1F~~
              35.20

S L Y _ P

113
114
~~122~~ 122
123
124

14

117

125

122 - 127

{ 9:15   SILVER CROSS
NEW Lenox
DR. LONGO

815 824 - 2106

6 - 60

_ E _ A D

D E _ A T

6050-1100-1008-2837-414

R E~~FAB~~   R E _ A P

E ` I S I

72230   O A^D

167
Site   C / A M E^O

            _ E _ A R

            4 _ _ I E

E _ R A

D E _ _ M

Made in the USA
Monee, IL
15 December 2019

6050-1100-1008-2837-414